FiSH!™
TALES

**Real-Life Stories to Help You Transform
Your Workplace and Your Life**

Stephen C. Lundin, Ph.D., John Christensen,
and Harry Paul, with Philip Strand

HODDER

MOBIUS

Hodder & Stoughton

First published by Hyperion in 2002
First published in Great Britain in 2002 by Hodder and Stoughton
A division of Hodder Headline

A CIP catalogue record for this title is available from the British Library

ISBN 0 340 82193 0 (hardcover)
ISBN 0 340 82439 5 (trade paperback)

Printed and bound in Great Britain by
Clays Ltd, St Ives plc

Hodder and Stoughton
A division of Hodder Headline
338 Euston Road
London NW1 3BH

CONTENTS

CONTENTS

INTRODUCTION

Over the last few years the story of a remarkable group of fishmongers from the Pike Place Fish market in Seattle has stimulated many of us to consider new possibilities for our work and our lives. As the poet David Whyte put it, we are finding ways to "make work a reward and not just a way to rewards." We are also finding ways to live our time on this planet full to the brim as a testament to the preciousness of life.

The story of these unusual fish guys was told in the book *FISH!* In it we described four principles that help foster a great life at work—"Play," "Make Their Day," "Be There," and "Choose Your Attitude." These principles are a part of what we call the FISH! Philosophy. Living this philosophy results in a workplace where the quality of life is satisfying and meaningful, and the experience for customers, internal and external, is compelling.

The core message of the book you are now holding, *FISH! TALES*, is that a richer and more rewarding life may simply be a few choices away from where you are right now. Each of the first four sections in this book features a real-life story that highlights one of the four FISH! principles. Still, the other principles also are depicted in each feature story. It must be this way. Play, for example, operates in a context of being there, making someone's day, and choosing your attitude. It is the context that keeps play appropriate.

After each main story are several short stories—we call

them "small bites"—to further illustrate the main principle. Feel free to sample these at random.

If your spirit is inspired by the real-life stories in this book, we hope your actions will be guided by the 12 weeks of transformational activities at the end of *FISH! TALES*.

Throughout this book, Steve Lundin will be your guide and narrator. You will hear his voice and perspective, in first person, as he tells the story of FISH!, introduces the four feature stories, and takes you through the 12 weeks of activities.

The rest of us join in at various other times. Phil Strand wrote the feature stories. John Christensen and Harry Paul contributed their considerable experience working with the FISH! Philosophy and shared their insights.

Now, let's go fishing!

FISH!™
TALES

The Fundamentals of FISH!

John Christensen and I, each in our own way, have been curious about what is possible at work. I worked at a camp for children with serious physical challenges for six summers. After banging around the "real" world for many years I came to realize that Camp Courage was one of the most joyous workplaces I had ever experienced. I began to wonder why organizations full of able-bodied people were often so joyless.

John brought a social-service background and an artist's eye to the world of work. He was intensely curious about the occasional workplace he encountered that exuded an abundance of energy and passion. He would come back to the office with a story of a shoemaker who was passionate about his work or a furniture company with a spirit that soared. We found we were both searching for an image that would help inspire all of us to see what was possible at work, knowing we all are destined to spend a majority of our lives there.

In 1997, John and I flew to Seattle and hauled our film gear to the quaint little town of Langley on Whidbey Island. There we filmed the poet David Whyte, who is known for the message he shares with organizations about bringing one's whole self to work. We became immersed in conversations about wholeheartedness in the workplace. David quoted a friend of his who said, "The antidote to exhaustion is not necessarily rest. The antidote to exhaustion is wholeheartedness. It is those things you do halfheartedly that really wear you out."

Later, talking to the camera, David recalled an answer he gave on a radio interview when asked what it was like to take his message into organizations. He responded, "Sometimes it is quite marvelous and sometimes it is like visiting the prison population." When he said this I was surprised and shocked. Then he continued, "I don't mean organizations or businesses are necessarily prisons, but sometimes we make prisons of them by the way we live there."

Our time with David was a feast for the soul. We left Whidbey Island with a greater understanding about this as-yet theoretical workplace image we sought.

We drove back to Seattle and spent Friday night there. I was flying out the next morning, but John was staying until the following night. We asked the concierge to suggest places a guy from Minnesota might visit on Saturday. She recommended the Pike Place Market. We knew little about Seattle and this seemed like a fine idea, since John loves to shop.

John was on one end of the market when he heard laughing and screaming. Like a child following the Pied Piper, he was drawn to the sound, and found himself in the back of an enthusiastic crowd. Suddenly the crowd parted and he came face-to-face with the source of the commotion. It was the World Famous Pike Place Fish market.

If you've ever been to Pike Place Fish, you know that when a customer places an order, the fishmongers standing in front of the counter throw the fish over the counter to coworkers for wrapping. They make some spectacular catches and the crowd loves it. The fishmongers regularly invite delighted customers behind the counter to try their luck at catching.

But on this day, as John stood in the middle of a cheering crowd, he was more interested in the way the fishmongers threw themselves into their work. The market was crowded and noisy, but when one of the fishmongers focused on a customer, it was like they were the only two people in the place. Everywhere John looked, both employees and customers were smiling, laughing, and most important, connecting with each other. Not coincidentally, the cash registers were ringing like crazy.

John watched in fascination for almost an hour. Suddenly a fishmonger broke his trance. "Hi!" he said. "My name's Shawn." His hair was red, his smile was huge, and his eyes twinkled mischievously.

"What's going on here?" John asked.

Shawn answered with a question of his own. "Did you eat lunch today?"

"Yeah," John said, wondering what he was getting at.

"How was the service?" Shawn asked.

John shrugged his shoulders. "Okay, I guess."

"But did the waiter really connect with you?"

Connect with me? What in the heck is he talking about? John thought to himself.

Shawn's eyes locked on John's. "See, this is our moment together, yours and mine, and I want it to be like you and I are best friends."

John started to understand what was happening here. A bunch of fishmongers—not MBA professors or organizational gurus—were showing him how to bring more fun, passion, focus, and commitment to work.

As John continued to watch the fishmongers engage and connect with customers, a drama off to the side caught his attention. One of the fish guys had attached a crayfish to a young boy's pants. The boy was startled and began crying. The fishmonger got down on his knees and crawled over to the boy, who was clinging tightly to his mother, and asked first for forgiveness and then for a hug. The fish guy had misjudged this child, but his recovery spoke volumes.

John's mind drifted back to the previous week, when he had taken his daughter, who has severe asthma, to the doctor because she was having trouble breathing. As they stood in front of the registration desk, Kelsey gasping for each breath, a cold voice asked them a number of questions. Its owner typed the responses, never looking up, and then barked, "Take a seat."

Finally a disembodied voice from the hall shouted, "Kelsey Christensen." The nurse, barely looking at Kelsey, carelessly whacked the top of her head with the measuring device attached to the scale. The nurse marched down the hall as John and Kelsey struggled to catch up, then stopped by a door and pointed inside, never looking back.

John looked at the boy at the fish market, who was now smiling and holding the crayfish. *Why would a fishmonger give more care to a frightened child than the professionals in the health-care clinic where I took Kelsey?* he wondered.

John watched one fishmonger after another engage customers with all the attentiveness of the best caregiver. He knew he had to capture this image on film. His intuition told him it would be hard to watch these guys at work, see the power of the way they live each day, and not be inspired. He suddenly felt anxious. What if they said no? Two hours later he had finally gotten to the point where he was ready to broach the subject with the owner. He said he was a filmmaker and before he could continue, one of the guys said, "Where have you been? We have been waiting for you."

ChartHouse Learning soon brought its cameras to Pike Place Fish. After watching hours of footage, we saw that the fishmongers created their engaging environment through a few fundamentals—simple but powerful choices that we all can make. We translated these actions into a new language we call the FISH! Philosophy. We explored four of the principles in a documentary-style video called *FISH!* They include:

PLAY— *Work made fun gets done, especially when we choose to do serious tasks in a lighthearted, spontaneous way. Play is not just an activity; it's a state of mind that brings new energy to the tasks at hand and sparks creative solutions.*

MAKE THEIR DAY— *When you "make someone's day" (or moment) through a small kindness or unforgettable engagement, you can turn even routine encounters into special memories.*

BE THERE— *The glue in our humanity is in being fully present for one another. Being there also is a great way to practice wholeheartedness and fight burnout, for it is those halfhearted tasks you perform while juggling other things that wear you out.*

CHOOSE YOUR ATTITUDE— *When you look for the worst you will find it everywhere. When you learn you have the power to choose your response to what life brings, you can look for the best and find opportunities you never imagined possible. If you find yourself with an attitude that is not what you want it to be, you can choose a new one.*

A year after the *FISH!* video came out, we explored these principles further in a book we also called *FISH!* (Pretty tricky, huh?) We invented a story about a workplace where people were so disconnected from their work that their department was known as the "Toxic Energy Dump." The book illustrated how the lessons of the fish market could apply to typical organizational challenges.

Over the next few years, through the film and the book, the FISH! Philosophy spread into organizations around the world. People began to reinvent what their time at work could be about, and the passion, energy, and accountability they discovered led to surprising business improvements. They shared their inspiring stories with us and, through their experiences, our understanding of what is possible through these principles expanded and deepened. You will find some of these stories in this book.

The people in these stories are no different from you or me. What makes them extraordinary is that one day they each made the choice to try to live more joyfully, responsibly, and wholeheartedly. The next day they chose again. And the day after that and the day after that . . .

Section One—PLAY

Play is not just an activity; it's a state of mind that brings new energy and sparks creativity.

Remember this old warning? "Boys and girls, playtime is over, get back to work." Most of us learned early in life that work and play are separate, and that if you are playing you could not possibly be working. But to have a livable work environment, one in which human beings thrive, a certain amount of playfulness or lightheartedness is required. We have found no exception to this rule. The alternative is what Ken Blanchard refers to as an "epidemic of tight underwear." Not a pleasant image.

An innovative environment demands even more play. Habitually following the direct "all business" line from Point A to Point B may *seem* more efficient, but it constricts one's capacity to generate new solutions when needed. The freedom to be playful—to take a winding, curious line—expands creative opportunities (as well as the minds and spirits of the humans involved). The spirit that allows people to wear a goofy tie or to laugh out loud without fearing what others think is the same spirit that encourages them to consider new ideas which expand the boundaries of what they used to think was possible. Creativity becomes an adult game of make-believe ("Hey, what if . . . ?") we can all play.

The fishmongers know that play can stimulate creativity. When a customer placed an order, they used to walk from behind the counter to pick up the fish, then had to hike all the way back around to wrap the fish and ring up the purchase. But one day they did something different. One of the fish guys threw a salmon over the counter to another. Eureka! Not only did they create a new kind of performance art, but they became more productive by eliminating a lot of walking back and forth.

Despite the benefits of a lighthearted workplace, it's amazing how much fear the thought of play strikes into the heart of management. When an executive for a large fast-food chain said, "You want us to tell 300,000 teenagers they can play?" he probably imagined the world's largest food fight.

One reason for the fear may be that we aren't sure what play is. The same people who are drawn to the playfulness of Pike Place Fish often can't imagine how they could ever replicate such an atmosphere in their own workplace. "What can *we* throw at work?" they ask.

The fishmongers have the answer. "There are a million different ways of playing," they say. "It doesn't have to be throwing a fish!"

Actuaries, teachers, or engineers will find different ways to be playful than the fish guys. That is the point. Play is not restricted to a toy or a game. It is the lighthearted feeling you release inside people when they are enthused, committed, and free of fear. A successful budget meeting in which serious work is being done can stimulate the same feeling as a picnic.

SEND ME YOUR IMPLEMENTATION MANUAL FOR PLAY

Three weeks prior to a sales meeting at which we were to introduce the FISH! Philosophy, we received an unusual request: "We have all 57 branches coming to this meeting and we want our people to be more playful at work, but could you send your objectives for play? Or maybe you could send an implementation manual to show us how to play."

At first I thought he was joking. Can you imagine telling your children to go out to play, and having them say, "Great! What are the objectives?" But that didn't matter to the caller. He wanted nothing less than predetermined outcomes from this "play thing."

How could I help him understand? "What about some bullet points?" I suggested.

"Anything to help explain the play thing."

So I sent a whole flip-chart sheet full of bullet points. No words, just bullet points. Suddenly he got it! Play can't be implemented or rolled out to all 57 branches like a new accounting system. (My colleague Carr Hagerman makes this point well. Preparing to juggle knives or tools, he says, "You can play with an implement, but you can't implement play.")

Play must come from within and so you can only *invite* play.

We need to create our objectives together as a team. By the way, the meeting went great—and those concerned about the "play thing" were the most receptive to a playful atmosphere.

Play also requires trust. You can try to duplicate what the fishmongers do on the surface, but if you don't have the shared commitment and trust that make playfulness possible at work, it may not happen.

A hospital wanted to invite more playfulness into its environment, but a supervisor wondered if employees could be counted on to "play" appropriately.

"You give me access to medications that can mean the difference between life and death for patients," a nurse responded. "But you don't trust me to play responsibly?"

Playfulness won't flourish in places where people spend more time trying *not* to do the wrong thing than they do searching for ways to do the right thing. People may "play" in such environments, but they will do it in secret or as a form as rebellion. (Quick, the boss is coming! Get his picture off the dartboard!)

But in healthy workplaces, where people are free to be passionate about their work and accountable to their teammates, play happens naturally. When it happens in a context of "be there," "make their day," and "choose your attitude," play *will* be appropriate and productive.

The following story is about an invitation to play that provided a breath of fresh air in a workplace that needed a little more life. As managers and employees built trust and accountability, people became free to play in a way that lightened their spirits *and* improved the business.

A Company That
Has Fun Connecting:
Sprint Global Connection Services

It seems like just another day at the Sprint Global Connection Services call center in Lenexa, Kansas, but the phone agents are all shook up. There's been an Elvis sighting in the parking lot.

Sure enough, a limousine stops in front of the call center's windows. Aaaaaaaahhhh! (Pause for breath) Aaaaaaahhhh! It's the King! Suddenly two Elvi Girls, with poodle skirts, bobby socks, and hair the size of Graceland, rush the King. One attaches herself to his ankles.

Inside the center, grown men and women are so moved by the sight of the King that they are in tears . . . from laughter. "Elvis" looks suspiciously like Don Freeman, manager of Sprint's call center in Phoenix, and one of the Elvi Girls bears a striking resemblance to Mary Hogan, manager of the Lenexa call center.

Lori Lockhart, director of Sprint Global Connection Services, shakes her head in amazement. A few years earlier, who could have believed that managers—you know, the corporate hall monitors—would show up for a meeting dressed like this?

But the customer service agents on the phones are loving every second of it, and though their customers on the other end of the line don't know what's going on, they can hear the enthusiasm and energy in the agents' voices.

As Elvis enters the center, "You ain't nothin' but a hound dog!" wails from the loudspeakers. Lori cringes at the thought of hearing Don—I mean, Elvis—sing. But he decides to lip-synch instead, and after he leaves the building, all Lori can say, in her easy drawl, is, "Thank yuh. Thank yuh very much."

STAYING CONNECTED

Sprint Global Connection Services helps Sprint's long-distance customers get connected around the world. More than 1,000 employees in seven call centers across the country—Sprint has more than 80,000 employees corporate-wide—provide a variety of services, including operator assistance, information, calling cards, prepaid calling cards, customer service for people buying prepaid cards, and directory assistance.

Five years ago, Lori Lockhart wasn't worried about Elvis leaving the building; she was concerned about the agents leaving. "Turnover was becoming a major challenge in our industry, and the long-distance business is so competitive," she says. "We knew if we didn't have a work environment people were excited about, they were going to go elsewhere."

At first glance, *exciting* is not the first word one would use to describe the duties of a call center phone agent. For many it's an entry-level job. Agents handle 500 to 800 calls per day, each one averaging 30 to 35 seconds. Most of the information needed to connect the call is in front of them on a computer screen. "People often master the job so quickly that it can become almost second nature," Mary Hogan says. "You start getting the same kinds of calls over and over, and the boredom factor can set in if you're not careful."

So how do you help employees stay focused through 800 calls a day? In 1997, Sprint thought the answer was to have a lot of rules. "In a competitive, high-pressure environment, there's a tendency to manage by taking over versus letting people do their jobs," Lori says.

Sprint had rules for what its agents could wear. "I can't tell you the number of hours we spent in staff meetings talking about the dress code," Mary says. "How short can a short skirt be? Are women wearing panty hose? You could wear every color of jeans except blue."

Sprint had rules for what you could read. "We knew people could read at their stations and still do a good job," Mary says. "But you could only read Sprint material. You know what happened—people were holding a Sprint publication but inside it was a sports or glamour magazine."

Sprint even had rules for how you could sit. "Ergonomics, you know," Mary says.

"We felt like the police," Lori says. "Instead of finding new ways to make money for the business, we were walking around checking on people all the time."

The more the managers pushed, the more the agents pushed back. According to Lori, "When I had my roundtable meetings with the agents, there was so much nitpicky stuff. *Why can't I put my foot up on the bench? Why can't I wear jeans on Tuesdays, not just Fridays?* I was getting blasted by the agents for things they felt made their environment more stressful."

The managers were feeling stressed too. "It was the way we'd done business for a long time," says Mary, who had been in the call center business since 1964. "We knew we needed to change. We just didn't know how."

In the fall of 1997, Lori and the call center managers attended a Sprint leadership conference. The speaker urged them to find the "radiating possibilities" in each employee. "We were always looking for reasons why people weren't doing their jobs," Lori says. "Why not look for the possibilities instead?"

They also listened to a speaker from Southwest Airlines talking about their famed culture of freedom, teamwork, and respect for individual employees. Five minutes into her speech, the speaker said, "Oh my goodness! Excuse me. I forgot something."

She ducked down behind the podium. When she came back up, she was wearing an inflatable hat shaped like an airplane. She wore it for the rest of her speech. Suddenly Lori, Mary, and the other managers got it: Time to lighten up.

LEAP OF FAITH

Lori and her team began to envision what a workplace looked like where people had fun while they worked hard.

From these discussions they created a culture statement of who they wanted to be:

> We are proud to be a supportive community with a feedback-rich environment that embraces change, values diversity and learns from our experiences. We thrive on creative and innovative ideas, which add value for Sprint customers, employees and shareholders. We achieve our goals because we are accountable for our contributions to Sprint. We have a passion to succeed together and celebrate our accomplishments.

They knew this wasn't going to happen overnight or even in a year; this was going to be a journey of three to five years.

"We didn't tell any of the higher-ups about this," Lori says. "We were going to do it because we knew it was the right thing to do. But I was scared. How was it going to work? Well, it was going to work by delivering results."

Everyone else was scared, too. "We said we're all going to hold hands and jump together," Lori remembers. "Because we needed to have a leap of faith that we're doing the right thing by changing the way we lead."

The team kicked off 1998 by announcing a new dress code: "Just don't wear anything that could be a safety hazard." They also allowed people to read whatever they wanted at their stations.

"The agents used to say we treated them like kids. Our goal was to create an adult environment," Mary says. "You know you are accountable for serving the customer. If you can't do more than one thing at a time, you need to choose not to read. But most agents can do more than one thing at a time, it keeps them engaged through a long day, and they do a better job."

The agents were happier, but Mary was still having trouble getting people to come in on weekends and nights at the call center in Lenexa, a Kansas City suburb, and a satellite center she manages in Kansas City. "People would call in sick during those times," she recalls. "As a result, we were having trouble meeting our goals for service levels, which measure how quickly the average call is answered."

Sprint launched a summer program called Managers Attack Service-Level Headaches (MASH). Late one night Mary and the supervisors decorated the centers like MASH units. They donned khaki shirts at work and provided incentives for working overtime, with Hogan Bucks good for special prizes. IV bottles, attached to overtime sign-up sheets, hung from the ceiling. Supervisors sent candy bars to agents via a remote-control jeep and organized impromptu contests.

People started smiling again and the call centers began to achieve their service-level goals. "We knew we were onto something when I started getting handwritten notes from the agents," says Mary. "They said things like 'I never would have believed in all my years that you would do something this fun for us. Thank you—and don't stop.'

"I think we knew intuitively what needed to be done but didn't have the courage to do it. Those notes gave us the courage."

PLAYING WITH A PURPOSE

When Lori and Mary saw the learning film *FISH!* in the fall of 1998, they turned to each other and said, almost in unison, "That's us!" In a job that could easily have become repetitious and predictable, the fishmongers chose to make it fun and always surprising. They teased customers with a mischievous look that said, "C'mon, tease me back!" Each of the fishmongers acted like an owner of the market. They worked as a team, but as individuals they didn't wait passively to be told what to do. They constantly tried new strategies to engage customers.

When the fishmongers played, it was with a purpose. One second they might be wiggling a fish head at a customer, in the next they were completely focused as that customer placed a large order. The day seemed to breeze by—and they sold a ton of fish.

Had Lori and her team introduced the FISH! Philosophy a few years earlier, the agents might have laughed and said, "OK, what's next?" "Everybody would have thought it was just another flavor of the month," says supervisor Donna Jenkins. "But things had been changing. With every new thing that we added and *didn't* take back, their trust in leadership grew."

First the call centers made FISH! part of their decor. Employees hung posters with the principles everywhere, and supervisors donned fishing vests as a daily reminder of the team's new commitment.

But more important, they made the principles part of their daily lives. "We bought plastic fish stringers and gave one to every employee," Mary recalls. "When supervisors observed agents on the phone demonstrating customer-focused behaviors, they recognized them by giving them fish made out of colored paper. We thought it was important that the supervisors write on the fish exactly what they saw the agent doing, so it reinforced the behavior.

"At the end of each quarter, we held a fishing tournament. We put all the paper fish in a tank. If your name was drawn you got to go fishing for prizes with a pole that had a magnet on the end. People loved it—and they got better at their jobs."

"SIR, THAT CALL IS FREE!"

The centers incorporated the four principles into their regular coaching sessions. "When we want to recognize an agent for great service, we call it a FISH! Tale," Lori explains. "If the customer didn't have a good experience, we call it The One That Got Away."

They look for opportunities to bring a lighter touch to their customer interactions. "One of our agents got a call from a customer wanting to make a collect call to an 800 number," Don explains. "The agent said, 'Sir, today we're going to give you that call for free.'"

They work hard to make the customer's day even when customers are calling with problems. "Our system is pretty automated, and when equipment doesn't work right, it's designed to send the call to our agents," Mary says. "Customers can be pretty unhappy when they call."

When that happens, says agent Rhonda Lynch, "the most important thing is your tone of voice. It's not a fake cheerfulness. It's something sincere in your voice that says, 'I'm really sorry you're having a problem. Let me see what I can do to help you out.'"

When that isn't enough, Sprint's agents choose to stay positive. "Sometimes customers are so upset they don't care how happy you are," says agent Marcia Leibold. "But I'm determined not to let them rile me. I do what I can to help, and by the end of the call, they say, 'You have a good day.'

"Some people call us because they're lonely. Often it's older people, and from something they say, you figure out that they don't have family. While I'm processing the call, they'll want to start up a conversation. From a business perspective I need to get to the next call, but I let them talk a little bit and I try to say something positive to let them know somebody out there cares about them."

And the agents found a way to be there for several hundred calls a day. "Sure, there are days when every call starts to sound the same," Lori says. "But the next call might be someone trying to get through to her grandmother who's ill or a business traveler who misses his wife and kids."

The next call might even be a matter of life or death. "An elderly woman had fallen and couldn't move," Rhonda recalls. "Somehow she got connected to us, but she couldn't dial 911 or tell us where she was. Another agent and I spent 30 minutes making long-distance calls to the police and fire departments in her area—I think it was New York. The other agent talked to her to keep her calm and I placed the calls. Finally we figured out where she was. The police had to break her door down.

"I know we helped saved that lady's life. When I went home that night, I knew I was doing worthwhile work."

HEARING SMILES

At the Lenexa center, Mary and her supervisors continued to look for ways to increase attendance on Friday and Saturday nights. "Many of our employees are 18 to 24 years old," Mary says. "They're the newer employees, so they get hours nobody else wants. We asked ourselves, 'Why wouldn't they want to be here on weekend nights?' Well, duh! They want to be out partying like the rest of the world."

Mary wheeled the stereo system from her office into the call center. "The center is so big we had to crank the speakers," she says, laughing. "At first nobody wanted to sit near the front."

But agents quickly jumped out of their chairs and started boogying while they were processing calls. "Before, if you had a really negative call, you didn't have a release to take your mind off it," explains agent James White. "You'd try but it was hard to shake that feeling for a while. The music gave you something else to focus on for a few seconds, and then you could go on to the next call and give that person your very best."

Mary's team carefully monitored calls during the first few weeks. "We were worried what customers would think of music in the background," she says. "But when we listened, we heard smiles in the agents' voices."

The Lenexa center got only one complaint. A woman called late one Friday night. Midway through the call, she said, "What's going on there? Are you having a party? Let me speak to your supervisor!"

The supervisor came on. "What's going on there?" the woman said suspiciously. "It sounds like a party."

"Yes, ma'am, that's kind of what we're doing," the supervisor said. "We are trying to create a fun atmosphere at work for our agents so they will be here Friday and Saturday nights so they can serve customers like you. I apologize if you don't like the music, but we're just trying to do some things because we care about our employees."

"Are you kidding me?" the woman said. "You'd do that for your employees?" The line was silent for a moment. "That's really nice," she said.

WHAT IF IT DOESN'T WORK?

Had Sprint received a complaint like that two years earlier, Mary says, "we would have apologized all over the place and shut down the whole thing. Heck, we might have shut it down if we had one *internal* complaint."

But part of Sprint's new culture statement talked about "learning from our experiences"—which meant taking risks. "In the past, when we'd talk about trying something new, people would say, 'Now, if this doesn't work, we'll be locked into it forever,'" says Mary. "We didn't want to do anything that could be called a failure, so we never did *anything*.

"Now we said, 'OK, let's call it something else. Let's "pilot" something. Let's "trial" something. It might work and it might not. But if it's something that might improve our culture, let's at least try.'"

Mary brought a toy box into the center, filled with foam discs, foam footballs, and soft toys for people to toss back and forth. "That was a real risk. What if someone gets hurt throwing things around? Now it's a Worker's Comp issue. Then we thought, 'We have established clear accountabilities. They know they have to do their jobs. Why don't we trust them? If something happens, the worst thing is we don't do it again.'

"So now people will sometimes toss stuff back and forth, and the young guys will toss the foam football to keep energized late at night. In three years, we have never had an issue with it. Oh, sometimes the guys get a little rambunctious late at night, but you just settle them down a bit."

The same thing happened when Mary installed a big-screen TV in the Lenexa center. "It makes it nice for the football and basketball fans working weekends. The first weekend the TV was in, one of the agents brought in a video.

"On Monday morning I came in and opened an e-mail that basically said, 'Oh Mary, we know we're in big trouble. We showed the movie and it had a scene that wasn't appropriate for the center and now we can't watch videos anymore!' I just laughed and told them, 'Well, I guess we'll be screening movies now.'

"In a positive work environment, it's not about taking

things away. It's about learning every day and finding solutions that allow people to have an energized culture."

Music is a big part of that culture now. "We decided we didn't want elevator music. We wanted upbeat music. But people have different tastes. We bought a bunch of CDs, almost every style, and told the agents, 'We're going to play your kind of music, but we're also going to play *other* people's music. That way it's something we can all enjoy.' It was a good way of teaching diversity."

STARTING RUMORS

In Sprint's more straitlaced days, the call centers occasionally tried to have fun. "We'd send out formal communications," Lori says. "We'd say, 'Hey, a fun thing is coming! We're gonna have fun Friday at 1 p.m.!'" The message, of course, was that it wasn't fun the rest of the time.

But at Sprint's call centers, it became increasingly difficult to predict what might happen, especially on Friday and Saturday nights. And the managers and supervisors led the way. On New Year's Eve, Mary showed up dressed like a baby. Sometimes she led agents in the Chicken Dance or Macarena. "If customers could have seen the weird stuff we were doing while processing their calls, they wouldn't have believed it," she says. "On the other hand, most of them probably would have joined in!" (The Chicken Dance eventually died a natural death. "People got tired of it. Maybe it's time for a comeback," she says with a wink.)

"Every week a new rumor would start up," Lori says. "The young agents would tell each other, 'Make sure you're working this weekend, because something crazy might happen.'"

One weekend Mary hung a small disco ball from the ceiling. All weekend the agents processed calls while listening to the likes of the Bee Gees and KC and the Sunshine Band and doing the Hustle. The weekend was such a hit that Mary installed two larger disco balls. "They don't rotate all the time," she says. "If we're a little sluggish, we turn off the lights, turn on the balls, and crank the music."

Sometimes the agents played bingo, with supervisors walking around displaying the numbers on a board. "When someone gets bingo, the supervisor takes 15 minutes of calls for them while they take a break," Mary says. "It's a good way for supervisors to keep up their call-processing skills."

At Sprint's call center in Jacksonville, Florida, one of the supervisors created a character called "Delightful Day." At least once a month she visited each customer agent station with her shocking outfits and greeting of "Helllewwwwww!" On July 4, Delightful Day showed up in a blue sequin dress with red trim and flags hanging from her hat.

All this activity occasionally made the managers nervous. One night at the Phoenix center, about 10 p.m., there was so much going on that Don Freeman became concerned that customers were hearing this. "So I started monitoring calls from my office," he says. "I listened to call after call and I got goosebumps.

"I wasn't hearing any of the craziness in the background. I

wasn't hearing lifeless, monotone "SprintmayIhelpyou" voices, either. I was hearing energized, alive 'Sprint! May I *help* you?' voices. It was so awesome I went down to the center floor and joined in."

Don began making regular appearances as Elvis with his guitar, while the agents pleaded with him not to quit his day job. He also redesigned the Phoenix center's physical environment to resemble a coffeehouse, with couches, pool tables, and high-speed Internet access, to appeal to the Arizona State students who made up a large part of their workforce. "A lot of the students come in early to work now just to hang out," Don says.

What might have happened at Sprint's call centers if leadership had only told people to play, instead of playing along with them? "We would have tried, but we would have always been looking over our shoulder, wondering, 'Are we going back to the old days?'" Rhonda says. "Sometimes when we get real busy, we don't have a lot of time to play, but at least we know it's not going away."

"IT'S NICE TO KNOW YOU'RE HUMAN!"

Part of creating a more adult atmosphere at Sprint's call centers was to give people choices. That meant giving people the choice *not* to play. "Sometimes people have a headache, don't like the music, or they want to study while they process calls," Mary says. "We have a separate room across the hall from the main center where there's no music or activities." Agents can go back and forth at any time during the day.

"Some of our folks feel if you're working hard, you shouldn't be having fun. It may be generational or just the way they were raised. Others say, 'This is cool,'" says Lori. "But it's not about having to participate in the music or games. For some people it's knitting something for your grandchild or your neighbor's baby, or drawing something you love—whatever it is that brings you joy so you can transfer that feeling to the customer.

"And if a supervisor hears a perfect call, they'll run out and do something zany and immediately recognize the agent. The other agents see it and are celebrating each other's success while still taking calls—which brings a smile when they're talking to the customer."

It's also about being yourself when you serve others. Each of the call centers do monthly quality surveys with agents to make sure their interactions with customers are up to expectations. "We used to have a form with dozens of questions, like 'How many times did you say please and thank you?'" Mary says. "If you didn't say thank you a certain number of times, we'd take points off. That really bugged the agents. They'd say, 'You are so nitpicky.'"

Sprint sought feedback from agents on the elements that comprised a great call and streamlined the form. "We still want people to be polite," says Mary. "But now we try to find opportunities to play or be there, instead of demanding automatic responses that may not always be appropriate."

In the process, Sprint replaced robot-like sameness with authenticity and individuality. "Sometimes we'll be laughing about something crazy, like Mary walking by wearing a pig nose," Marcia says, "and the customer will say, 'It's nice to know you're human!'"

MOMMY, WHY ARE YOU ACTING SO FUNNY?

One day, while attending Sprint's annual leadership conference, Lori Lockhart had an epiphany. She was having fun. She had dressed like a fish at a conference. She danced with Elvis and the Elvi Girls. "I finally felt comfortable that I could be myself," she explains. "I became more relaxed, more confident in my leadership abilities. I was having fun seeing results."

Then it hit her. "I'm living the FISH! Philosophy at work," she thought. "Why don't I take it home to my family?"

The first night she came home she decided to play, have fun, and be there instead of being tired, stressed, and irritable. "My daughters immediately saw this change in me. They said, 'Mommy, why are you acting so funny?'

"I told them, 'This is the new me and I'll try harder to be a better mommy and have more fun.' They told me that they thought I was wonderful before, but now I was the best mom in the universe!"

The next morning (this part of the day was typically filled with stress, sometimes tears, and always racing the clock), Lori tried to start the day with humor and play as she prepared for work. As her daughters walked her out to the car for the morning good-bye ritual, they had big grins on their faces and said, "Because of Mommy, it's going to be a great day and we're going to have fun today."

"Those words made my day," Lori says. "We really try not to sweat the small stuff. The other day my husband, Patrick, told me he was going to start choosing his attitude and dance while he's vacuuming. Great, honey, go for it."

CREATING OWNERSHIP, STIMULATING CREATIVITY

Sprint's call centers have always had an open-door policy. "But it didn't always feel like open door," agent Rhonda Lynch remembers, laughing. She holds her thumb and forefinger less than an inch apart. "It was open door . . . to a point."

Today, agents are an integral part of how the call centers plan. "We decided before launching any major changes we would do our homework and engage employees in those discussions," says Mary.

Each of the call centers has widely used feedback channels. Lori even has her own online feedback site. "I ask people to please tell me if something I'm doing is not living up to our culture." The feedback can be blunt, as when an agent told her to communicate more clearly and concisely. "I need that. I can't take action on something I'm not aware of."

Agents also play a major role in identifying opportunities for better performance. "Three years ago, I would have never had an agent come to me to present a new idea to improve a business result," says Lori. "Now I have meeting after meeting with agent teams who are presenting proposals on how we can improve call-handling efficiencies or customer satisfaction. Some of those proposals have saved big dollars."

In Phoenix, Don Freeman regularly invites agents to act as "Sprint board members" and tell him what they think the call center should be working on.

Leadership also has moved to more of an open-book management philosophy. "I talk a lot with employees about the challenges that keep me up at night," Lori says. "We talk about budgets, unit-cost targets, margin challenges, competition."

A few years ago, Lori believes, the agents wouldn't have cared. "Now there's a much keener interest at all levels of the organization in how the metrics work together—financial, customer satisfaction, employee performance. People understand how what they do every day helps to drive the business."

In the process, by playing with ideas, Sprint's employees unleashed a lot of unexplored creativity. "A lot of people don't think they have that ability," says Mary. "But once you realize we're not going to put limits on your mind, that we want you to brainstorm with us, you would be amazed what opens up. People who I never would have dreamed were creative have come up with wonderful ideas—and I think they've surprised themselves too."

And the more management and employees play together, the more barriers go down.

According to Lori: "It all builds confidence in people that 'If I say something to Lori or Mary or one of the supervisors, they will listen to me and do something, and if they can't, they'll tell me why.'"

"As supervisors, we really are committed to being fully present for each and every employee," Donna Jenkins adds.

"It feels like a family," says agent Marcia Leibold. "I feel more connected to the management team than I ever have."

That trust will be key to the future. "There is so much change going on," says Mary. "It used to be that every time we wanted to make a change, we had to go through these huge change-management cycles. For employees it can be like a grief cycle. We don't have time for these lengthy change cycles anymore. The more trust we build with employees, the more they feel confident about the quick shifts we may need to make."

In October 1999, Sprint and MCI WorldCom began merger talks. "The day of the announcement, our leadership team watched the business news with agents on our big-screen TV," says Mary. "We talked a lot with employees about what was happening."

The merger eventually fell through. But what really impressed Mary was the reaction of the agents. "Had this happened a few years earlier, there would have been so much fear. But because of the trust that had been built up, there was a calmness that boggled my mind."

AN ANSWER FOR "HMMM"

The first time Gary Owens, Sprint's vice president of service operations, visited the Lenexa call center after Mary had installed disco balls, a speaker system, and a big-screen TV, she stopped him as they were about to go into the center: "I said, 'Gary, I need to tell you about some changes we've made so you don't have a mild coronary.' He walked in and all he kept saying was, 'Hmmm . . . hmmm . . . hmmm.'"

Then Mary showed him the call center's numbers. It had met or exceeded every one of its goals for retention, service levels, productivity, customer satisfaction, and on and on. "If you had ever asked me about putting in disco balls, I would have said, 'No way,'" he told Mary months later. "But you can't argue with success."

Having recognized the success, Gary endorsed the approach for the entire organization, using Lori's team as an internal benchmark. Gary also changed the organization's vision statement to *We have fun working while delivering the ideal customer experience in consumer communications.*

The numbers for all of Sprint Global Connection Services were becoming more impressive. The first year they went after a 25 percent increase in retention and exceeded it. Since then they've maintained it.

"We've actually had folks looking at higher-paying jobs within Sprint and turning them down because they liked our environment so much," Mary says.

Call center productivity, which was already high, increased another 20 percent from 1997 to 2001, and Sprint's call centers won a number of customer satisfaction awards. The group sets tougher and tougher goals each year. "We've met all of them," Mary says.

But Mary had another way of assessing her call center's

progress. "Before, I would walk down the hallways and hear little complaints here and there. I'd see people frowning. When you see and hear that stuff all the time, you tend to filter it out and don't pay as much attention to it as you should.

"But as our culture changed, people became happier, upbeat, relaxed. When I walk down the hallways now and I see a frown or there's even a hint that a person has a complaint or problem, my radar goes up right away. I know it's not normal anymore. I deal with the issue immediately, which just means our workplace is going to be better."

LIVING THE PHILOSOPHY

Mary Hogan used to just carry reports. Now she has a bag of props. "Every morning when I walk through the center it's like I'm going on stage," she says. "You never know when I might walk out in pig slippers or kitten slippers or crank the music or grab somebody off their position and start dancing.

"I've been in the call center business 37 years and I am living proof that you can change. My management style today is nothing like it was a few years ago. The change has allowed me to show my human side to everybody. I am who I am and people can see it now. They can hear it too—because I'm usually laughing."

Mary has had opportunities to move into higher positions. "But I can't make myself move on. The past few years have been the most energizing of my career. I have so much passion for what we're doing.

"We have crossed so many lines. I don't know if there are any lines we *wouldn't* cross to try to improve the business. But when you launch on journeys, you have to get outside your comfort zone. It's not about seeking permission. We all have a certain sphere of influence. It's about taking risks within that sphere.

"It feels like *Star Trek*. We're boldly going where no one else has gone before."

SMALL BITES

⋊ᐃ MEMORIES ᐃ⋉

Is there any workplace where you *can't* play? How about a funeral home? Yet we heard this story from a funeral director: A family was sitting at the funeral home, lost in their grief. The funeral director suggested that they all join him in a circle and talk about the fun times they had had with their mother. Before long, laughter mixed with tears as they celebrated the joy and happiness she had brought into their lives.

⋊ᐃ THE LIGHTHEARTED TOUCH OF A CHILD ᐃ⋉

Why do so many flip charts have to look so boring? One woman decided to spice up her presentation by asking her kids to color her flip charts with crayons. Her coworkers loved the rainbow-splashed flip charts, and her playful presentation was a hit.

THE WIGGLE FACTOR

As John Christensen was about to pay for his purchases at a large discount store, he reached for the pen-on-a-chain to sign his check. Suddenly the pen wiggled out of his reach. The cashier was pulling on the end of the chain hidden underneath the counter. John laughed. So did the cashier. Every time John goes into one of these stores now, he hopes he'll be as engaged and delighted as he was by that cashier. Just in case, he also carries his own pen.

FUN IS FUNDAMENTAL

A new hospital, inspired by the fishmongers, decided to integrate play into its basic philosophy. Part of its mission statement reads, "We are dedicated to exceeding our customers' expectations in a compassionate and *fun* atmosphere." Its core values include quality, compassion, integrity, organized solid planning, teamwork, and *fun*.

Play and productivity go hand in hand in this hospital. On Beach Party Day, patients who are able toss a beach ball to each other. Little do they know this is physical therapy. If they were in the therapy room, they might not give much effort. The fun factor changes everything.

LIGHT UP SOME SMILES

Sure, "play" sounds great. But what if your workplace is a heavy manufacturing plant where safety is critical? First, any activity that puts someone at risk is *not* play. It's recklessness. But there are ways to lighten spirits even in the most demanding environments. During December at a tool manufacturing plant, the maintenance workers hung icicle lights on the chain-link fence surrounding the site. The machine operators asked if they could decorate too if they kept it safe. Garlands and twinkle lights began to appear wrapped around workbenches and conduit—anything that didn't move.

Play doesn't have to be a specific activity; sometimes it's a state of mind. And a state of mind is influenced by the environment you create.

WHO AM I TODAY?

Interviews are often intimidating, uncomfortable, and a good way to ruin the armpits of your best shirt. But an employment consultant at a major university has found a way to bring play into the process. She comes dressed according to the position for which the applicant is applying. If people are interviewing for construction jobs, she dresses as a construction worker, hard hat and all. If people are interviewing for security jobs, she dresses as a security guard. It puts the applicants at ease, introduces them to a culture of fun—and attracts people who will flourish there.

THE DECIDING FACTOR

Every company wants to attract the best employees, but you'd be surprised what draws them. A young computer talent chose his company because a miniature blimp was flying around the office when he interviewed there. The salary and benefits were competitive; he figured it would be more fun and professionally stimulating to work there.

✂ "IF YOU'D LIKE TO HEAR A DUCK QUACK, PRESS 7...." ✂

What can you do to attract employees? At one company, employees decorate job applications with crayons and welcome notes. Another company encourages employees to record entertaining phone messages, then suggests that potential hires call random staff numbers after hours to get a feel for how much fun it is to work there.

✂ A BIGGER PLAYING FIELD ✂

Before they felt it was safe to play, the employees of a large ski resort wanted to know how far they could go. "They wanted to know how big the playing field is," the CEO told us. "'If we step off the playing field you can call foul, but let's together define the size of the playing field.' I started with a relatively tight playing field—these are the rules. The employees said, 'No, we need an expanded playing field—expanded rules, a little more latitude, a little more trust.'"

So the CEO redrew the lines and made the playing field bigger. Now the resort holds impromptu karaoke contests on the mountains. Kids bob for crawdads. Guests do the limbo on their way to the chairlifts. Every ski resort in the area has the same beautiful mountains and amenities. This resort is trying to differentiate itself by freeing its people to create more playful, personalized experiences for its guests. How big is your playing field? Does it need to grow?

Section Two—MAKE THEIR DAY

The world becomes a better place the moment you act on an intention to serve another.

When you first walk into the World Famous Pike Place Fish market, you might think you are being entertained. The flying fish, shouts, chants, teasing of customers, and antics are entertaining. But you come to realize that you have walked onto a stage and have become a member of the cast. The fish guys are sizing you up and just waiting for an opportunity to throw you a line. They are committed to recreating their vision of the market each day. But that can only happen if they find a way to make a memory for you so that when you leave, whether you are carrying a fish or not, you leave with something you will want to share with others. Then those others will themselves come to the market. And they too will leave with a memory. More will come. The word will spread as the ripples go out. And more will come. . . . You get the picture.

At the center of the incredible success of Pike Place Fish is the engagement of one person at a time. It bears repeating.

They are not selling fish; they are making the world a better place to live, one engagement at a time. By the way, they sell a lot of fish.

An opportunity arose one day to introduce a friend and supporter to the market. I had heard he would be in Seattle on business and suggested he make his first visit the market while in town.

At about 3:45 on a Thursday afternoon, Ken arrived at the market and stood in the back row enjoying the energy and the action. A thought crossed his mind and his face must have telegraphed it ever so slightly. It was the only opening Sammy needed as he approached Ken and said, "May I help you?"

"I was thinking that smoked salmon would be great at a family get-together this weekend. What would you suggest?"

"I think you should sample a couple different kinds," suggested Sammy.

Five minutes and three kinds of salmon later, Sammy asked for a commitment and Ken made his choice, decided on an amount, and gave Sammy his credit card. Sammy went back to the credit card machine gingerly holding the card. A moment later he returned with a serious, concerned look. "Do you have another card, Ken?"

Ken experienced an unusual emotion; he was flustered, and he frantically searched for cash or another card. After he had dug in his pockets for what must have seemed an eternity, Sammy spoke up.

"I was just curious, Ken. I don't need one."

Ken was so caught up in the moment that he missed this cue. Finally Sammy said, "I don't need another credit card, Ken. I just wondered if you had one."

Ken's face broke into a giant grin. He had just experienced a playful engagement and a lasting memory was formed. The ripples go out from that moment every time Ken tells that story. Listeners smile when they hear it and many find their way to the market to collect their own memories. And the ripples go out in larger numbers. And people come to the market to collect their own stories. And on and on . . .

After Ken left the market we told the guys that it was Ken Blanchard, author of many best-selling business books including *The One-Minute Manager*. They said, "Who is Ken Blanchard?" They had simply treated him the way they treat any willing customer.

There is nothing quite as powerful as turning your attention away from yourself and asking how you might connect with another human being, customer, family member, or colleague and "make their day." Or as Justin at the market says, "At least make their moment."

The next story is about a car dealership committed to making each customer visit a memorable one. That's not an easy task, given the way many people feel about having to haggle over a vehicle. But it became a task transformed once the employees of Rochester Ford Toyota began a journey to discover how to focus on other people's needs, not their own.

Driven to Serve Others:
Rochester Ford Toyota

The lot at Rochester Ford Toyota is filled with hundreds of vehicles, but right now Rob Gregory is interested in just one: a NASCAR racing car that's visiting his car dealership as part of a promotion. "Just listen to that," he says lovingly as its engine roars.

For a few seconds, Rob is the boy from Grand Forks, North Dakota, who used to love shopping for cars with his father. "I thought it was the best thing in the world," he says.

As he grew up, he learned that many people felt differently. "If it's a choice between getting teeth pulled and buying a car, the dentist gets the first call."

But when Rob first took a job selling cars in Grand Forks in 1987, he met a man with a different vision. Wes Rydell's western jackets and bandana neckties gave him the appearance of a Hollywood cowboy, and his maverick ideas set him apart from the herd. "His vision went something like this: 'Do the exact opposite of what the rest of our industry is doing and you'll be close,'" Rob recalls.

"Mr. Rydell talked about being a 10, reaching your fullest

potential. People want to be a 10. They want their marriage to be a 10. Companies want to be a 10. From a business perspective, how do you start on that path?

"Mr. Rydell believed there are five areas essential to every business's success: 1) Customer enthusiasm, 2) Employee satisfaction, 3) Ability to generate profits, 4) Growing market, and 5) Continuous improvement. All five are necessary conditions, but you can only pick one as your favorite."

Most car dealerships chose to be driven by 3—profits—but Rydell decided to focus on 1—customer enthusiasm. "Any one of these isn't necessarily better or worse than any other is," Rob says. "But when you focus on customers first, it puts you on a different journey. You stop focusing on what *you* want and start focusing on what the people you are serving want.

"Mr. Rydell said, 'When a friend of mind comes in, I make sure they get the best deal possible. What would happen if I treated every customer as if they were my friend?'"

From this perspective, Rydell created a new vision for his dealerships: *To Be So Effective That We Are Able to Be Helpful to Others*. "If you get really good at what you do, who would come to you to be served?" Rob asks. "Everybody would. The more people you are truly serving, how do you feel? You feel great!

"Yes, you need to stay focused on profit. But is it a cause or an effect? If you ask people if they want to be a millionaire, everyone says yes. But if you ask *why* they want to be a millionaire, the underlying reason always comes down to this: They want to be happy. The only way to be happy in this life is to get outside yourself and serve others. That's the journey Mr. Rydell was trying to get me on."

WHAT ARE YOU FEEDING?

When Rob bought Universal Ford Toyota in Rochester, Minnesota, in November 1999, many employees weren't feeling especially happy.

"It had a reputation as a typical car dealership—come in, get beat up," recalls Al Utesch, Universal's parts manager for several years. "Most people worked hard for the customer, but the main goal was financial. Our customer satisfaction scores were among the worst in our region, and employee satisfaction was so low it was almost immeasurable."

"I saw a lot of people pay high prices, and those who didn't negotiated until they were blue in the face," says John Davids, who had joined the sales staff six months before Rob purchased the dealership.

Even the dealership's profitability was misleading. The economy had been robust for several years and Rochester— home of the Mayo Clinic, one of the world's leading medical centers—was a prosperous community. "The previous ownership would have given itself an A in profitability, but in terms of the market's potential, it was really a C," Rob says.

Rob was not surprised, but neither was he judgmental. "Ownership chose to emphasize 3 (profit), not 1 (customer satisfaction)," he said. "The owner lived out of town and saw the dealership as an investment, not a mission. If you lived out of town and got a big check every month, what would you change?"

But when you build an environment based on take, that's what you feed in even well-intentioned people. Customers come in with their defenses up. Salespeople try to make as much as they can on each car because they think they might never see the customer again. Management tries to squeeze profits from every corner, and employees focus on what they can get, not on what they can give.

The dealership's decision to run sales, service, and parts as three distinct financial entities created—unintentionally—an environment in which coworkers saw each other as competitors. "With the emphasis on the bottom line, we blamed each other for everything," says Julie Sweningson, parts manager. "It got so bad that we would refer our friends to other dealerships if they wanted to buy a car, and sales would refer their customers to other parts stores because they said we were difficult to work with."

No one, including ownership, felt good about the situation, but no one knew quite how to change it. Profits seemed good and, as Wes Rydell had said, your focus determines the way you see the world.

"I talked to a lot of people individually when we came, and there was some drama, some victim language," remembers Brian Kopek, who moved to Rochester Ford Toyota with Rob as new-car sales manager. "If we had a rallying cry, it would have been, 'I'm gonna get mine.'"

Rob made one major external change, renaming the dealership "Rochester Ford Toyota," but he told the employees that the most important change needed was an internal one.

"How is everything working for us?" Rob asked. "If we keep doing what we're doing, will things get better or worse?"

The answer was almost unanimous: "Worse."

"And how is everything working for you personally? Is your work doing for you what you hoped it would?"

The room was quiet.

Rob called for a new journey. "What if we put the customer's needs before our needs?" he said. "What does the customer really want?"

Do they want to negotiate with several people to get the lowest price or do they want to know our price up front? Up front. "OK, no more negotiating or pressure tactics," Rob said. "We'll post our best possible price on every vehicle. It'll be like playing poker with our cards showing; we'd better have a pretty good hand."

And does the customer ever want to buy a bad car? No. "OK, anyone who buys a used car from us gets their money back in seven days," Rob said. "If they bring it back within 30 days, they can exchange it for any used vehicle of equal or greater value."

Does the customer want to deal with salespeople who are paid to sell or paid to serve? Paid to serve. "OK, our salespeople will be paid per each unit sold, not a percentage of what they negotiate on each vehicle."

By lowering the price of each vehicle, Rob was asking his staff to sell twice as many cars for the same amount of money.

"You can either try to make a lot on a little, or a little on a lot," he said. "I believe it was Sam Walton who said, 'A little bit on a lot is *still* a lot.'"

But all Rob's staff heard him saying was, "We're going to work twice as hard, and we might go broke, and you might make the same salary—I think you'll actually make more—but you *could* get happy along the way!"

Only a few employees liked the sound of that. Most held their breath and waited to see what would happen. Some quit.

A PHILOSOPHY, NOT A PROGRAM

Had any business succeeded by focusing on what Rob was asking of his employees? Well, yes, he explained, a fish market had.

He told them the story of Pike Place Fish and its vision of becoming world famous. The fishmongers didn't get into that journey simply because they wanted to sell more fish. They just wanted to be happier. When they looked outside of themselves and concentrated on helping other people, they discovered a satisfaction they had not imagined possible. As they served more people, more people came to them to be served. How did they feel? They felt great.

Some employees at Rochester Ford Toyota thought what the fishmongers were doing was amazing—exactly what they had been looking for. Some thought it was amusing. Some thought it was obvious. Some thought it was BS.

"To most people it looked a lot better than their current

reality," Rob says. "So we had a choice. Should we take some personal responsibility and try to change our environment, or should we keep waiting for the solution to arrive on a silver platter?"

Initially they threw stuff to each other, joked with customers, did ballet moves across the showroom floor—"anything to add levity to drudgery," Rob says. "Obviously the old way wasn't working and people were willing to listen. Plus when you own the place, some people will pretend to care even if they don't."

"The excitement seemed to be there, mostly in the showroom, but I think some people were still terrified, so whatever leadership did, they were going to do," Brian recalls.

A few months after assuming ownership of the dealership, Rob attended an employee culture meeting. "I'm thinking 1-2-3-4-5 is working, the whole thing is working, and a few people said, 'Do you realize nothing has really changed around here?'

"Well, some things were changing. But if from your point of view it hasn't changed, you haven't changed. So they were actually confessing that they hadn't changed. Basically they were saying, 'One more time, Rob, let me get this straight: I have to sell twice as many cars to make the same salary . . . but I'm going to feel better? It doesn't feel too good today!'"

Rob realized at that moment that the journey was just beginning. He had thought 1-2-3-4-5 and the FISH! Philosophy would fix everything and everyone—instantly. "But nothing gets fixed until we choose to fix ourselves. They had implemented all kinds of programs at the store to try to fix it, but they came and went. That's what people thought this was."

Rob saw that these principles are a philosophy, not a program. A philosophy is not implemented; it is explored, chosen, believed, and practiced. Some people at the dealership were already practicing these principles; for others the decision to embrace them might come 10 minutes later, a month later, maybe even years later.

"If you give a squirt gun to people who don't trust you, then say, 'Have fun!', of course they're going to think you're full of it. First we needed to build trust and accountability. People need to see you are committed to something more than just a program of the month."

Not long after, Rob was looking at copy for two proposed billboards, both of them standard brand messages, such as One Low Price! "I was trying to decide between the two, and it popped into my head. In 10 seconds I drew it out: 'Have You Tried Our Fish?'"

A few managers were helping Rob select the final billboard. They saw the first two billboard ideas. No and no.

"Check this out," Rob said. He showed them what he had just drawn.

They all pointed to it and said, "That's it!"

"WE ACTUALLY HAD FUN. . . ."

Rochester Ford Toyota's new billboard went up, just across the highway from the dealership, in March 2000. The first day a woman called and asked what kind of fish they were selling; Brian started thinking they should put a small case of salmon in the dealership.

Some people were suspicious. "Customers would call up and say, 'What does that mean? Is there something fishy going on? Are you trying to fish us in?'" recalls sales associate Sam Grosso.

The sales staff hadn't paid much attention to the billboard. But the prospect of customers descending on the showroom asking about this cryptic message suddenly commanded their attention. "How are we supposed to respond to that?" they said.

But when they thought through it, it wasn't that hard. "What works in the fish business works in the car business," Sam says. "Serve people, make it fun, have a good attitude, be there when you're needed. Most people understood that."

The hardest part was convincing customers that Rochester Ford Toyota was serious: the price on the car *was* actually the price. "People come in prepared for battle and there is no battle," Sam says.

One by one, several of the salespeople started to let go of their fear. It wasn't easy, but they stopped thinking about the money and started thinking about the other person's needs. Selling a car stopped being a chess match in which each player tried to anticipate the other's next move, and became a conversation about the customer's needs.

Customers noticed. "Before, you'd get lines from the salesman like, 'Now, I wouldn't do this for everybody,'" a customer said on the showroom floor one day. "Yeah, right. I can just hear the salesman thinking, 'Because out of the 30,000 people I see each year, sir, I can honestly tell you that *you* are special.'

"But there was none of that here. They explained all of the options and additional coverage with absolutely no exaggerating attempts to make you feel you should get it. Just 'Here are the advantages. Here are the disadvantages. Let me know how I can help.' I was here when it was Universal, and I can tell you, it's an entirely different place."

Soon customers started writing letters that said things like: "We actually had fun purchasing this car."

"Provided me with the service and kindness of a friend. . . ."

"Being a widow, I did wonder how you would treat me. I received top attention, indicating I was important. . . ."

"I had commented with my coworkers about the car-shopping experience—just wishing and wanting the effort to be straightforward, honest, pleasant, and short-lived. Then I came on a fluke to Rochester Ford Toyota and found the characteristics I thought could not exist. . . ."

"I'm young and female, but I was treated with complete and total respect. . . ."

"This is the best car-buying experience I have ever had, and I have probably bought 25 to 30 vehicles in my lifetime."

Months earlier, when Rob had introduced the new commission approach, several members of the sales force, Sam Grosso included, had thought seriously about leaving. Some top producers did. But Rob convinced those who stayed to give him six months, and their sales increased dramatically. "It worked," Sam says. "It just makes things easier when you're not worrying if people think they got a good deal or they got the same deal as their neighbor. I'm having a good time now. My old customers see the difference in me."

One day Rob stopped by to say hello to a customer—a large, intimidating man—who was completing a purchase with salesman Howard Hawk. "I hate car dealers," the man growled, then smiled. "This will be the first place I ever bought a car without having to cuss somebody out."

SELLING WHAT THEY NEED

Not long after, the staff watched a video featuring John Miller on personal accountability. In it Miller told how he once requested lemonade in a restaurant. "I'm sorry," the young waiter said, "we don't sell lemonade." Five minutes later the waiter placed a glass of lemonade on Miller's table.

Miller was confused. "I thought you didn't sell lemonade."

"We don't," the waiter responded, grinning. "I sent my manager to a store around the corner to get it for you."

A few days later a customer came into the Rochester Ford Toyota showroom. One of the salespeople asked if he'd like something to drink. "What I'd really like is a cappuccino," the man said jokingly.

"We didn't have cappuccino," Rob says. "So our salesperson says to himself, 'Let's see if this is for real.' While he showed the customer around, one of the other guys drove over to a convenience store, grabbed a cappuccino, and brought it back for him."

The customer couldn't believe it. And he bought a car. But all the sales staff could talk about was the delighted look on the customer's face.

Skilled salespeople have always known how to make customers comfortable. "How could I ask you for a big profit over dealer cost and get you to buy from me, unless you laughed or I somehow got you to enjoy the process?" says sales associate Dan Kocer.

But a shift began to happen. "Now when you talk to people, the first thing in your mind isn't how much money am I going to make on this customer because I need to make a house payment," Dan says. "You know something's going to come out of it—if not a relationship, then at least a better feeling about how you're treating people."

The true test came when people automatically started doing what they didn't need to do. Instead of just pointing people to the parts department, they escorted them there. Instead of leaving the customer in a room alone while they checked out her trade-in, they invited her to ride along. When they saw a mother simultaneously coping with a fussy baby and trying to find the service department for an oil change, they volunteered to drive her truck there and get the process started.

John Davids tried to make people's day by doing things for which he didn't get paid, like making sure accessories were added so the vehicle was ready when the customer wanted it. "It all starts with attitude," he says. "Even helpful, good-natured people need to check their attitudes every day, because it's easy to worry about the money first. Just be willing to come in and serve every day. We can actually build friendships now. The other day a customer from out of town invited me to dinner. How can you beat that?"

"It's not everybody's thing, but when some people pick up their vehicles, we make it an event. We have all the salespeople step out and give a round of applause; everybody thanks them, we give them roses and balloons," Brian Kopek says. "And people cry. My gosh! How do you explain that?

"When you're in business every day, you tend to think, 'It's *just* a car!' Maybe they've been treated terribly in the past. We need to remember that we're selling people something they need for their lives. They need that car to go to the hospital, to go on vacation, to pick their kids up from school.

"When customers get emotional like that, Rob will get a little choked up. He has to walk away. He'll say, 'I think I saw some garbage on the lot. I better go pick it up.'"

LITTLE THINGS

If you look up the word *calm* in the dictionary, you'll find Lloyd Hyberger's picture. "I'm pretty easygoing," he says. "I don't get too worked up about anything."

Maybe that's why Lloyd, a sales associate at Rochester Ford Toyota, doesn't mind lending his car to customers whose own vehicles are in the shop. "If a customer is in a pinch I sometimes let them take my personal vehicle to work. They bring it back when they pick up their car. If something happens, that's what insurance is for.

"I'm a pretty relaxed guy, and I want other people to feel relaxed. I've got a little fan in my office and if somebody comes in on a hot day, I turn it in their direction a bit to take the sweat off their brow."

The mercury was considerably lower one night when Lloyd got a call at the showroom. "It was pretty bitter, a typical Minnesota winter night," he remembers. The caller lived in Dubuque, Iowa, but she was staying at a hotel a few miles away near the Mayo Clinic, where her husband was receiving leukemia treatments.

The woman's car was already in the Rochester Ford Toyota shop for repairs. She was worried enough about her husband; she was tired of worrying about their car. "I want to look for a new car," she said.

Lloyd told her to take a taxi. He said he'd pay for it. He warmed up a car and drove her around the lot until she found the vehicle she wanted. "We had already appraised her other car. We cleaned up the new car for her, transferred her belongings from her old car. She wasn't sure how to get back to the hotel, so I drew her a little map." By the time Lloyd was finished, it was more than an hour past closing time.

The woman returned the next day. She was not alone. She had told her husband about how she had been treated, and he had left his hospital bed because he wanted to thank Lloyd.

Several weeks later Lloyd got a letter from the woman. "When my courageous husband was fighting leukemia at Mayo and our car broke down, you treated me so honestly and compassionately that my husband wanted to meet you," she wrote. "He shook your hand one month before he died."

"We just did what we were supposed to do," Lloyd says. "But I sure felt good about it." His quiet voice softens even more. "Gosh, I think about that just about every day."

CHANGE YOURSELF

Even as the environment at Rochester Ford Toyota changed, there were days when Rob wanted it to change even faster. "I love quick fixes. It's part of my nature as a human being. I want what I want when I want it," he says. "See, one of my frustrations is that I think I have this gift: I can see what's wrong with everyone else.

"But if you want to change the world, first you have to change yourself. That has been very humbling, because I realized that nine out of ten problems in my organization, it's always been me. Now I see that. So as I work on myself, I find I have a bigger impact than when I was trying to work on other people."

So Rob worked on himself. He began to learn to listen. "There are times when Rob doesn't like what you have to say about how he's handled a situation or talked to someone, but he will reflect on it, come back, and sincerely be appreciative," says Al Utesch.

He began to learn to give his employees freedom. "Deep down, if I'm honest with myself, I know I still measure things by money," Rob notes. "So when people make decisions that have financial repercussions, it's difficult for me not to shoot the messenger or fire at will.

"But we have a card with our values on it, and it says, 'We have nothing of greater value than our people.' So what does that look like in practice? Would you be patient while your employees learned if you truly valued people? The answer is, 'Of course.'"

Rob also learned, more and more, to be led by the organization's vision, not short-term considerations. "One of Lloyd's customers calls us up," he recalls. "He's going out to Idaho. The truck he bought from us is acting up in a blizzard in South Dakota. He's at another dealership and he says they can't fix it today. I said, 'If they can't, pick a vehicle on their lot, load your stuff in it, and I'll just buy it from them for you when you get back.' Well, the dealer fixed the truck; I think they saw how committed we were and their pride got involved.

"That guy didn't just buy a vehicle from us. He bought our reputation."

JUMPING IN WITH BOTH FEET

As Rob started changing himself, others decided to join him on that lifelong journey—people like Al Utesch. The parts manager, who had started out washing cars at the dealership 29 years earlier, had thought about leaving. But there was something in this belief about getting outside yourself that sounded a lot like what his parents had taught him and what he was teaching his own children.

Then the service manager resigned. Rob felt Al was the best candidate for the job, though not everyone else did—Al included. "After 29 years in parts, I was in a comfort zone," he says. "I was scared to death. I spent the first two months sweating at night."

Rob says Al jumped in with both feet. "He never even checked to see if the water was cold or hot. He never even asked about pay."

In Al's opinion, the department's commitment to customer service was a joke. "We talked about the issues and how to fix them. Some guys had been beaten up so much in the past they wanted to quit, but they decided to give the new way a chance."

But other employees wanted no part of it. "They were some key players, but they didn't want to line up philosophically with the direction we were going," recalls Rob. "They were choosing not to be here. Knowing they'd produce a profit, I, as the owner, looked at Al and said, 'Are you sure?' Al pointed to our philosophy, mission, and values card. I said, 'OK, you're sure. Move on.'"

To replace those who left, Al hired several people who had never been service advisors before. He took people with high energy—positive people, customer-oriented people—and trained the necessary skills.

He also redesigned the service area. "We used to open the doors at 6:45 a.m. Two lanes, customers bumping into each other. It was like herding cattle." Al changed it to a single lane, with reservations every 15 minutes. "The goal was to give more personalized, quality time with the customer so the advisor can accurately report what the problem is."

In a few months, the service department's customer satisfaction scores soared in the top 10 percent in its region. Profits and market share rose significantly. Employee satisfaction made the biggest jump Rob had ever seen. "Before, we just fixed *cars*," Al says. "Now we realize that we're taking care of *people*."

"There are days when I'm down and I don't believe," Rob says. "Now Al comes and pumps me up, and I remember, Oh yeah! What we do *does* matter!"

MR. PERFECT

The first time Chuck Dery, the body shop manager, heard about the dealership's new philosophy, he told Rob it was BS. "I told him that a lot," he says. "There's no way a person can come in and tell me this fish story, and if we just do this, this is what will happen. I finally thought I'd try it, just to prove Rob wrong. But it backfired on me. Things kept getting better and better."

That's when Chuck became Mr. Perfect. "People would come up to me and say, 'How are you doing?' I'd say, 'Perfect.' They'd say, 'You can't be perfect.' Why wouldn't I be?

"If I let myself have a bad day, I'll go out and ruin every one of the guys in my department in about 10 seconds. Not a problem. If I come in with a grudge, or I had a fight with my wife, and let it affect me, I might as well take production and shut it down, because I'm the guy they look to.

"The quality of our work is the same as it always was. It was always good. The difference is attitude. If people are down, I coach 'em. Every situation's different. Maybe a guy has an argument with his wife and I'm the marriage counselor. I'm there for them and I get 120 percent back.

"When you're on the phone and somebody asks how you are, say 'Perfect.' I guarantee you people will call you on it. 'No, you can't be perfect.' I say every day is a perfect day. Feels better just sayin' it. I got 10 or 12 of my buddies saying it; it's all they say now. 'Perfect.'"

PLAYING YOUR PART

Julie Sweningson, parts manager, used to go to lunch with two service technicians. "All we did was complain about other people," she recalls.

Then one of the guys asked, "What do the other people say about me?"

Julie shook her head.

"No, come on," he said. "I can take it."

Julie told him, and it turned out he couldn't take it. "We stopped going to lunch after that."

Working in auto parts can be a thankless job. "You only hear the bad things if a part is back ordered and the customer is inconvenienced," she says. "People don't see everything you do to help them, locating parts, jumping through hoops."

But she stopped thinking about what she was getting and started focusing on what she was giving. "In the past, if a part was back ordered and we had quoted the customer a price, we'd just say you'll have to wait. Now if we quote a price, then find the part at another dealership, it's gonna cost us more and we don't make as much on it, but we get it anyway, to satisfy the customer. Short-term cost, long-term gain.

"You know, I don't understand how it works, but it does. The work is actually harder now, because we're busier. We have the same number of people cranking out the same number of parts, but we're enjoying it.

"I'd like to say I'm a lot different, but sometimes I slip back into that defensive mode. But I'm not as defensive. I'm calmer. Rob's shared a lot of ideas with us, and it's great to get that training. A raise wouldn't have helped my attitude at all. I've seen that done. You give a person a raise, but they still have a bad attitude. Here we are giving people the opportunity to change themselves, and that's better."

MAKING A DIFFERENCE

When Wayne Brueske's father owned a service station in Rochester, he rarely advertised. "He felt if he could not exist on word of mouth, he didn't deserve to be in business," says Wayne.

Growing up around cars, Wayne became a skilled mechanic. He joined Universal Ford in 1980. Like his father he was concerned about his customers, but by the late 1990s, he had begun to believe that management—under the fifth owner he had worked for—was not as concerned. "Everything was money, money, money."

Wayne didn't feel Universal cared much about its employees, either. Convincing management to buy tools and equipment that saved time—as well as the technicians' backs and knees—was a constant battle.

The battle wore on his attitude. One day he taped his employee number over the name on his shirt. "The service manager was really upset, but I figured I was just a number to them."

Wayne tried not to let his attitude affect his work, but it affected his outlook on almost everything else. He went to lunch with Julie Sweningson, complained, and walked around with his head down. "I was down in a hole so far I couldn't see light, much less touch it. It was to the point where either I left or I was gonna start having physical problems."

He had two other jobs lined up when Rob bought the dealership. When he heard Rob's initial talk, he said to himself, "Even if he does half of what he says, we'll be better off. Focusing on the customer was one of my values, and I thought, 'If I take another job, is it really going to change me? Or am I just taking my attitude to a different job?'"

Wayne stayed, but his attitude did not change overnight. When he and Rob had a run-in over one of Wayne's complaints—changing uniform companies—Rob said, "If it's so bad here, maybe you should move on."

It could have ended there, but both knew that would have been the easy way out. Rob offered to meet with Wayne and the other technicians every week. No other owner had ever made such an offer.

"At first I thought it was a chance to get some issues resolved in the shop," says Wayne. "It didn't turn out quite the way I envisioned it, but I guess I'm better off for the way it turned out. Mostly Rob talked about our values and how when we get outside of ourselves we can get around the other stuff."

Rob learned too. "I think getting inside their heads, them getting inside mine, seeing what I deal with and what they deal with, it helped us focus on what we had in common," he says.

"Before, I was probably scared to say what I really felt. Not knowing how it would be taken by management, I was afraid of losing my job," Wayne says. "But sitting down and talking with Rob, I feel we can talk about anything, without anything being held against each other."

Wayne chose to recapture something that he had hidden inside himself. "I started going out of my way, more than I used to, to make sure that people know I appreciate the little things they do to make my life easier or funnier or happier," he says. He joined an employee culture committee to find ways to recognize employees. One of their ideas was an appreciation card.

On the day the cards arrived at the dealership, Al Utesch decided to do something about some unruly shrubs on the south side of the showroom. Everyone had been complaining about how they looked. It was hot and sticky, but Al trimmed the shrubs. When he went into his office later, he discovered one of the cards. It said: *Thank you. You made a difference today*.

The card was from Wayne. "It may seem strange, a bunch of guys in a garage giving cards to each other, but it made my day," Al says.

Wayne knew that his journey would not always be smooth, and he knew that he, like others, would create bumps along the way. But now he had a vision of what his workplace *could* be.

In his spare time, Wayne volunteers with the Olmsted County Sheriff's Dive Team, searching ponds, lakes, and rivers for missing swimmers and evidence. One week they searched for a 13-year-old boy last seen at a swimming pond.

"We searched all day Saturday, but the water was really muddy and we called off the search at midnight," he recalls. "It was a terrible feeling. We searched Sunday. Nothing. Finally, on Monday, we found the body. All I could think about is how much I have to be thankful for. I've got a young son. I can still tuck him in tonight."

At a meeting with the service technicians that week, Rob talked about the dive team as a metaphor for work and life. "He said we don't swim around in murky water not knowing what we're going to find next because it's easy," Wayne says. "We do it because in the end we know that what we do every day makes a difference."

ONE DAY AT A TIME

By the spring of 2001, Rochester Ford Toyota was still early into its cultural journey. "A lot of people are on board, but it's a constant struggle," Brian Kopek says. "There are days when people call and tell us, 'You're no different than you were.' Swing and a miss. So we have to move forward with great patience, forgiveness, and understanding."

But the people of Rochester Ford Toyota had taken some important steps. In each of the five key areas of its philosophy—customer enthusiasm, employee satisfaction, financial performance, market effectiveness, and ongoing improvement—it had improved dramatically.

The dealership's "Have You Tried Our Fish?" billboard had been up for a year, and Rob—not unlike many leaders who shift from one "solution" to another—thought it was time to change it. "For me, FISH! had become a checkmark," he said. "It was like, OK, now our employees have a better sense of the journey. Let's check off the FISH! Philosophy. Done. Time to move on."

But when he suggested a new billboard, the managers looked at him like he was crazy. "Are you saying that as a culture, we truly understand the power of choosing our attitude?" they asked.

"No, not every day."

"And you believe that as a culture we are truly living in the present? We have no fear of the past, we don't fear the future, and we are always there for others?"

"Not always . . . not yet," Rob said.

"Do you think as a culture we completely understand the real energy that we will get in life from getting outside ourselves and truly helping other people?"

"Uhh . . . no."

"And you'd consider that this is an environment where play is a natural extension of a culture with high levels of trust and accountability?"

"No."

"And you are ready to move on?"

"Well, uh, no," Rob said. "I was . . . um, just saying if we ever did think about moving on . . ."

Rochester Ford Toyota finally did put up a new billboard. It read "Gone Fish" and it listed four points: "1. Play— Make It Fun; 2. Make Their Day— Go M.A.D. (Make a Difference); 3. Be There— Right Here, Right Now; and 4. Choose Your Attitude— Make Your Choice."

"They quickly pulled me back to staying the course. Discipline has never excited me. To live our vision, to live the FISH! Philosophy, is all about the art of discipline. I have faith in the values and in the people who are attracted to those values that we will always have more than we need. But I, being a human being and a skeptic, say, 'Well, sure, it's worked *so* far—but what *else* should we be doing?'

"There really is nothing else. We should continue to work on our vision and values every day."

SMALL BITES

✄ *YOU* COULD BE NEXT ✄

The Play Committee at one information systems department has come up with lots of fun activities. They've decorated the walls with butcher paper and invited employees to create their own graffiti (the only rule is no obscenities) and sponsored an Easter egg decorating contest and a name-the-baby-picture contest. But their most memorable stunt happens every few weeks, when one member of the department comes into her or his office to find that it has been decorated and she or he is the "Person of the Day." No one but the Play Committee knows who the next honoree will be.

What better way to remember the importance of making someone else's day than to have your colleagues make yours?

✄ PAIN RELIEF FOR APRIL 15 ✄

How could you resist a tax preparation office that offers free aspirin? During tax season, the office does its best to give even customers who owe money a smile. All the staff members dress casually to keep out any "stiff" attitude. They give children lollipops and toys, and even dogs are welcome in the office. They also offer customers beer and wine to relieve their misery—it's just a joke, but it usually gets a laugh. This tiny office has just three tax preparers, and some office backup, but they complete over 2,000 returns in less than 10 weeks each spring.

᙭ "THE WHEELS ON THE BUS GO ROUND AND ROUND. . . ." ᙭

Remember riding the school bus as a kid? The driver often ignored you; you just hoped the bullies did too. Here's how the supervisor of safety and training for a large metropolitan school district in Colorado makes the ride fun and memorable.

Whenever he drives the school bus, he acknowledges every student that boards the bus. Randomly, as a student boards, he'll ask the student for his or her bus pass (his district doesn't use passes) just to get a reaction. When the kids respond that they don't have one, he says, "Well, you will just have to take a seat and have fun."

When the bus is almost full, he tells the kids to sing "Happy Birthday" to the next kid who gets on the bus. The reaction is always priceless. Sometimes he will ask a student with really cool shoes what size they are, and would she mind trading for the day?

The driver says the students enjoy this type of humor. He also is letting them know that he notices them and cares about them. He has had to discipline students much less often and they are having a lot more fun on their 77-passenger yellow limousine.

ANOTHER SCHOOL BUS DRIVER STORY!

A 140-employee company that provides school bus services has always had a policy of not allowing children at interviews. But one day the hiring director got a call from a woman who wanted to interview for a school bus driver job and needed to bring her two young children. The hiring director said, "I love kids! Bring them with you!" The interview went great and the applicant said, "Any company that loves children so much must be a good place to work." Recruitment and retention are two of the biggest challenges facing the bus industry; to meet that challenge, it takes people, like this hiring director, who are willing to bend the rules.

FLEECING THE CUSTOMER

Making someone's day is often about the element of surprise. At an optical store, an employee was visiting with a woman while her husband got his eyes examined. The woman mentioned that she spent much of her time sewing for her small grandchildren. "I used to sew for people all the time too," the employee said. "I have some Christmas sweatshirt fleece I'd love to give away." The customer thought it sounded great but couldn't believe she was serious. But within a few days, the customer had received the free fleece in the mail.

ᕉ   **A SMALL RED RIBBON**   ᕉ

In the days following the horror of September 11, 2001, it was pretty quiet in most workplaces. Many people, especially those of us who live far from New York or Washington, D.C., wondered, "What can *I* do to help?" So we donated money. We gave blood.

The day after the attacks, P.J., one of our colleagues, went to a fast-food restaurant. She was greeted by the manager, who was holding a spool of red ribbon. The woman cut a small piece of ribbon and asked P.J. if it was OK to pin it on her. P.J. watched the manager pin ribbons on dozens of people—office workers, high school students, construction workers. For a moment, people who ordinarily would have dashed in and out, barely acknowledging one another, were connected.

ᕉ   **CODE "SWIM"**   ᕉ

Remember the hospital where fun is one of its core values? When a patient is discharged, a Code Swim is called—meaning the patient is "swimming" away. The staff gathers in the hall and gives them a grand send-off, complete with hugs and, almost always, tears.

ᕉ   **LET THEM EAT CAKE**   ᕉ

Harry Paul has a son who plays baseball. At the end of the season it is customary to provide treats for the team. His wife,

Mary, prepared a delicious chocolate sheet cake with a thick chocolate frosting and Harry was drafted to deliver the cake, paper plates, napkins, and plastic utensils.

As the game ended and the sweaty players assembled in their soiled uniforms for a treat, Harry looked at them and then at the paper plates he was holding. On the spur of the moment he said, "We can cut this cake in little squares and serve it with napkins—or we can just dive in."

The players said, "We would like it on plates with plastic forks and napkins, Mr. Paul. Not!"

Twelve pairs of hands reached for heaping handfuls of cake. As Harry picked up the pieces, the startled coach was being chased around the baseball diamond by 11 boys and one girl wanting to share their good fortune.

Section Three—BE THERE

You can multi-task with "stuff," but you need to "be there" for people.

At Pike Place Fish the fishmongers have learned that customers want your full attention when you are with them. A big part of their magic is being fully present.

How much do you actually get done when you are in one place thinking about a different place? Why not commit to being in one place at a time? When you are present—not dwelling on what happened in the past or worried about what may happen in the future—you are fully attuned to opportunities that develop and to the needs of the people you encounter. You gain a healthier perspective and the capacity for greater focus and creativity.

In no line of work is "being there" more important than in health care. When you try to provide the best possible patient care while simultaneously attempting to reduce costs and deal with constant change, a stressful workplace can be the consequence. That's why this field offers important lessons for all industries and situations.

"Be There" means be present—fully present—*especially* when you are interacting with another person. If that person happens to be vulnerable, your ability to be present can have both positive and healing effects. Patients in hospitals and clinics, residents of nursing homes, those living in homes for the developmentally disabled, and children all share a high level of vulnerability. The capacity of caregivers to "be there" for the people they serve is perhaps the single most powerful quality-of-care variable. If you doubt that for a second, simply remember how you felt the last time someone gave you her or his undivided attention.

DAD

A few years ago my dad had a massive stroke. He lives in a nursing home now. While he needs total care and can't speak in a way that is understandable, he understands everything and is quite verbal.

It is hard to staff nursing homes. The work can be unpleasant and depressing, and the pay marginal. Hence the nursing homes in the Minneapolis area are often the first place of employment for new workers who come to town. At the home where Dad resides this is certainly the case. One day a new aide came into Dad's room to get him ready for the day. As she proceeded to get Dad dressed and toileted, she conversed with him in a way that made him the center of her universe. The fact that he could not be understood didn't seem to bother her as she went about her job. You could see his counte-nance lighten as she spoke with him.

I have seen others come into Dad's room, often wearing white uniforms, and I have watched them continue to talk with their colleagues in the hall as they went about their rou-tine tasks. I could literally see Dad tense up. According to his record, at times like this he actually says a word or two that is quite clear.

Unconsciously these staff members treated Dad as if he were a person who had only physical needs—and they per-formed required tasks with him and nothing more. The new minimum-wage aide performed her tasks equally well. But she acted with a wisdom that took into consideration that Dad has a soul and spirit also, and she nurtured these by *who* she was *being* while she went about her work.

"I DON'T HAVE TIME!"

Carr Hagerman, a gifted speaker who works at Chart-House Learning, was talking with a group of nurses when one of them loudly proclaimed she did not have time for all this stuff. She said she was too busy already. But another nurse im-mediately said, "I don't think we are talking about doing any-thing extra. I think this is about *who* we are being while we are doing the things we need to do anyway. When we are with a patient we can be *physically* present or we can be *fully* present. The difference to the patient is considerable. How much of the stuff we are distracted by as we work with a patient actually gets done anyway? So why not be fully present while we are doing the things we have to do anyway?"

The nurses sat in silence pondering the wisdom of their colleague then launched into a high-energy discussion about being there for patients—physically, emotionally, and spiritually—and how that is their tradition as nurses.

What follows is the story of a remarkable group of health care professionals who have transformed a part of the hospital system in which they work by devoting themselves to the idea of being there for their patients and for each other.

The Gift of Being Present:
Missouri Baptist Medical Center

Shari Bommarito, R.N., became a nurse because she wanted to be there for the whole person—emotionally *and* physically. "I once cared for a patient whose cancer was terminal," she says. "His wife could not stand to see him suffer and wanted to turn the ventilator off, but didn't want him to know. He wanted to turn the ventilator off, but thought he needed to keep fighting for his wife's sake.

"I had enough time back then on my shift to talk to them and figure this out. I sat them down together and I said, 'You should tell each other how you really feel.' They were holding hands when I closed the curtain. Finally she came out and said, 'He is ready to die.'"

Sometimes nursing is about profound moments, and sometimes it is about pills and bedpans, but it is *always* about being there for people who need you.

But while medical care has improved dramatically from a technical standpoint and nurses are better trained, there are fewer opportunities to be there for people's emotional needs. Spending time with the patient has been replaced by the need to spend time monitoring technology. Hospital stays are shorter and the list of tasks that must be completed during that time is longer.

"Holding hands comes last on the list," Shari said. "If you get to it, great, but if you don't, that's the way it is."

"I HATE THIS"

On a sweltering summer day in 1999, Shari sat in her daily traffic jam. Her knuckles were white. She had a headache. She was recently divorced, one of her children had just been diagnosed with asthma, and she was working full-time again. Being away from her kids made the hour's drive to work every day even more frustrating. "I hate this," she said to herself, and suddenly the words, "Missouri Baptist" came into her mind.

At the time, Shari was a clinical nurse educator at Barnes-Jewish Hospital in St. Louis, Missouri. Barnes-Jewish is one of the best hospitals in the country (*U.S. News & World Report* ranked it seventh in 2000) and the anchor of BJC HealthCare, the area's largest health system. "It's high tech and high speed," Shari explains. "You see things happening there you don't see in other hospitals."

Missouri Baptist Medical Center, located in western St. Louis County, had recently joined BJC HealthCare. It was much smaller than Barnes-Jewish, though its cancer, heart, and orthopedics centers were highly regarded, and the number of births at the hospital would quadruple over the next two years. Missouri Baptist was also located five minutes from Shari's home.

Despite her doubts about leaving Barnes-Jewish—to Shari it seemed like the center of the world—she interviewed at Missouri Baptist and was hired as a clinical nurse educator. Her job: to make sure the nursing staff had the resources they needed to remain clinically competent.

She came to work her first day "scared to death," but during her tour, almost everyone she passed smiled, made eye contact, and said hello. Shari was a little uncomfortable at first. At Barnes-Jewish the half-mile-long hallways teemed with people on the run, and there never seemed to be enough time to greet people.

"These people are almost *too* nice," she said to her guide with a laugh.

"That is an expectation," the guide said. "You stop to help people when they are lost, say hello to people, smile, just be friendly."

"Wow, I can do this," Shari thought. Then, at lunch, a nurse asked her where she would be working.

"Fifth floor neuro-renal."

"Oh my, you have *that* floor?" the nurse said.

Shari's nervousness returned. "No one says something like that to you on your first day," she thought. "What have I walked into?"

After lunch Shari went up to the fifth floor. She was greeted warmly by the unit's head nurse, Hilda VanNatta, R.N.

She took Shari's hands in hers. "I am glad you are here." Shari nodded. "Hilda looks tired," she thought to herself.

FEELING THE PRESSURE

Missouri Baptist has always had a reputation for having a compassionate nursing staff. "I have always had caring people on this floor," Hilda says. "One Thanksgiving, when two of my staff got off work, they brought a special dinner to a woman who had no family, and gave up their own evening to spend the holiday with her."

But even caring people can feel the pressure of working on a floor like neuro-renal. "We take care of people with strokes, multiple sclerosis, brain tumors, seizures. Some have had surgery," explains Hilda. "The renal patients are complicated because their kidney failure has caused so many other problems. Many come to us every six weeks or so for dialysis; they're known as the 'Frequent Flyers.'"

"A few years ago many of these patients would have been in intensive care," says Cathy Flora, R.N., neuro-renal clinical nurse manager. "Now our staff's technical skills are a lot higher and we have the technology to care for them on this floor."

Nearly all of the patients on neuro-renal are so ill and weak they can't sit or stand on their own. It takes two or three nurses to lift, move, and bathe them, even to feed them. "Because some patients are in isolation rooms, every time you go in you have to put on a gown and mask," Shari said. "Once you are in, if you need something, you need another nurse to bring it to you, or you have to take everything off, get what you need, then put it all back on again. So you rely on others a lot."

In the fall of 1999, the number of tasks was growing and time seemed to be shrinking. "The mindset was, 'I get my tasks done before I help anybody else,'" Shari says. "I would see people standing in the halls with gowns on, looking for people to help them. When people did help each other, they weren't acknowledging or thanking each other. The thought was, 'You're doing your job. Why should I thank you?'"

Sharon Sanders, R.N., who had recently become a nurse, knew that her coworkers were caring people. "I didn't think people were always helpful or supportive of each other," she says. "People were focusing on the negative side of every-thing—not always—but I was pretty discouraged coming on the floor sometimes. Then again, being a new nurse, I thought, 'I guess this is what the real world is like.'"

A "FISHY" INVITATION

Hilda and Cathy agreed that their staff desperately needed help with teamwork. Before planning the training, Shari Bommarito asked the staff how they felt they were performing in six areas: teamwork, positive team attitude, communication, support for others, satisfaction working within the team, and having a say within the team.

Just 30 percent felt a strong presence of teamwork. Only a third of the staff felt strongly that there was good communica-tion among team members, and just 25 percent felt strongly that there was support for team members, a positive team attitude, and satisfaction working within the team. Only 15 percent felt strongly that they had a say within their team.

In other words, only 15 to 30 percent of the staff really liked their jobs. Hilda was willing to consider almost any solution. Shari suggested an unlikely one—the FISH! Philosophy, which she learned about at Barnes-Jewish Hospital. "We needed teamwork, and the only thing I knew for certain was that it was about teamwork," Shari says.

Shari created flyers with a picture of a fish dressed like a clown, juggling stars, clams, and crabs, and the words, "There's Something Fishy Going On Here . . ." She posted the flyers throughout the floor, giving people a few days to wonder what in the heck this was about. Then she invited everyone who worked on the floor—nurses, nurse assistants, doctors, housekeepers—to learn about the FISH! Philosophy. Most important, she mentioned she would be serving homemade cheesecake.

They came in groups of 10, usually just before their shifts or after. Shari showed a tape of the fishmongers. She explained that what they do every day—staying present and attuned to people's needs, doing something special for people, taking responsibility for their attitude even on the toughest days, and finding ways to enjoy their day—is what being a nurse is all about.

She pointed to Justin, a young fishmonger, who, when asked about his positive attitude, said: "It's a simple choice."

"Did you hear what he said?" Shari asked. "He's a 24-year-old kid and he's *choosing* to make a difference in the lives of people who are buying fish! If he can do it, we can choose to make a difference in the lives of people who are sick and dying."

Then Shari told about her drive to and from work. It was construction season, lanes were torn up, and the traffic was so busy it was almost impossible to get onto the road. "On the way home I stop at every gas station and let people pull onto the road in front of me. They wave and their kids blow kisses at me. I'm happy for them because I understand what it's like to wait.

"That's the idea. Take time to be there for people. Do something nice for someone else. When they say thank you, it feels so good you will want to find someone else to help."

Not everyone was convinced. One nurse, sure that this was another "program" designed to drain more effort out of the staff, said, "What do they want from us now?"

"*They* don't want anything," Shari responded. "*They* want you to enjoy what you're doing for others. *They* want you to have fun. *They* want you to stay. What do *you* want?"

The nurse was silent. "I want the same thing," she finally said.

THE GREAT FISH GIVEAWAY

At the end of each class, Shari gave each person a small plastic fish. She had found them in a novelty catalog and cut a slit in each fish's tail so it fit on employee badges.

"When someone does something nice for you, give them

your fish," she told the staff. "If you need more fish, I have plenty."

Before long, the staff was handing out fish everywhere. When people were overwhelmed, their coworkers started saying, "Let me do this treatment for you." Housekeepers helped nurses feed patients when no one else was available. People did favors for others on their breaks. "We started feeling like a team working together instead of everybody doing their own thing," Cathy said.

When Shari went to the cafeteria one day, she saw that the cashier was wearing a fish. "I don't know what it's for, but a nurse gave it to me," the cashier said. "She said I was being nice."

"Now you can give it to someone who does something nice for you," Shari said.

The cashier nodded in understanding. "Yep," she said.

According to Sharon Sanders, the plastic fish was an ice-breaker. "Sometimes adults have a hard time saying, 'You did a good job,' or 'I appreciate what you did for me,'" she says. "We hadn't been saying that to each other. Now we were."

The fish also gave real-time feedback. "Nurses are task-oriented," explains Cathy. "They want and need to hear specific praise for specific things."

If some people initially helped others because they wanted a plastic fish, the real reward soon became apparent. "Making someone's day is not just being pleasant," Shari Bommarito says. "It's about going out of your way to do something for another person. It's like an endorphin; it feels so good, you want to do more."

And in the process, the staff learned things they never knew about each other. "One of our secretaries kind of intimidated me," Shari said. "But I was so wrong about her. She would go out of her way to do anything for anyone. People started giving her fish and she started collecting them. She hooked her fish together and soon she had a chain of fish a foot-and-a-half long."

PLAYING WHILE SICK

The nurses also gave plastic fish to their patients. "If patients were a little crabby, I'd give them a fish and say, 'Here's a friend to keep you happy,'" Sharon Sanders said. "One man had a string of seven or eight little fish, and they accidentally got thrown in the laundry. He was pretty upset, and we replaced his fish in a hurry."

Carol Johnson, R.N., gave a fish to a patient who had made an extraordinary effort in his therapy that day. "He acted like I had given him a million dollars," she says.

Even some unlikely patients responded. "We had a dialysis patient who was extremely depressed," Cathy says. "That's a problem for many of our patients, but this woman was young and she had kids at home. She had a lot to live for and she was about to give up. She just lay in bed and did nothing.

"Hilda and I started giving her fish to get her to participate in her treatment. First we gave her plastic fish, then stuffed fish. Soon she started getting out of bed and began to progress on her own, and she started asking for fish when she did. I can't say what turned her around, but the fish were part of it. She really talked about her fish and showed them to people who came by."

At the same time, Shari Bommarito began noticing more nurses spending more time sitting with patients. "Usually you'd go in with a clipboard and stand over them," she says. "But I saw them sitting so they could get down to the patient's eye level. That little thing meant a lot, especially to our older patients."

Many patients began asking for fish, so they could give them to staff when they were extra nice or helpful. Some patients and family members wrote thank-you notes to the nurses on fish stationery.

And before anyone realized it, people on a floor full of sick and dying patients were smiling and playing with one another. "I'm playful—that's just me—so I just brought it to work with me," Sharon Sanders says. "Before, I hadn't been comfortable with that side of myself in the workplace. I didn't know it was acceptable to act that way. But I think we should try to make people's lives happy, whether it's in the middle of their life or the end."

She understands how important that is. Several years ago, her husband, Scot, was diagnosed with leukemia. At the time they had three small children. After having been a stay-at-home mom for several years, Sharon became a nurse. "I've had to deal with a lot of hard things, but you have got to live each day to the fullest and be the happiest that you can every day," she says. "I can't imagine living any other way."

COMPETING FOR STICKERS

Shari Bommarito returned from a two-week vacation in January 2000. When she came off the elevator on the fifth floor, all she could see were fish. There were fish hanging from the ceiling, fish magnets in patient rooms, and a poster on the wall that said FISH TEAMS.

"I'm walking down the hall wondering what happened," she says. "When I open the door to Hilda and Cathy's office, they're giggling! They had been talking about how to prepare for a visit from representatives of the Joint Commission on Accreditation of Health Care Organizations."

"We had about 200 items on a checklist, and I wasn't sure how to do it," Hilda explains. "One morning I was reading the Bible about Moses and how he didn't know how he was going to get everything done to get the Israelites to the Promised Land. His father-in-law, Jethro, said you need to form teams and get everyone involved. That gave me an idea."

Hilda and Cathy organized several teams. Each team had eight or nine people, including one physician. Each team appointed captains and named itself after a fish. Names included Barracudas, Purple Tangs, Angelfish, Piranhas, and Night Groupers.

Hilda and Cathy issued a friendly challenge. Teams whose members completed certain tasks, such as finishing their self-study packets for accreditation, would receive stickers. At the end of three months, the team with the most stickers would get a party and prizes.

To help the teams learn what they needed to, Hilda and Cathy created contests. One featured fish-shaped pieces of paper with questions about various aspects of patient care. When staff members wrote the answer on the bottom of the paper, their team got points for stickers. Teams competed to make posters to help educate coworkers on infrequently prescribed medications. As teams accumulated stickers, they also accumulated knowledge that would help them provide better, more efficient patient care.

"The fish teams found a lot of ways to improve," Shari said. "One of our physicians complained that his patients' blood sugar [levels] weren't always being documented in the right place on the chart, and when they weren't he had to go hunting for it. One of the teams asked the doctor if they could use his picture. He was a good sport. They superimposed his head on a cartoon picture of King Neptune and printed on it, *Please Document Your Blood Sugars!* They posted copies everywhere on the floor. The nurses laughed, but they also started documenting blood sugars correctly."

In the process, play boosted productivity. "We really wanted those stickers," Sharon Sanders says. "We were like little kids. We would stand at the chart and say to each other, 'Look, my team has seven stickers and yours only has four.'"

THE CLARINET AND THE CONDUCTOR

When Leo Carter, a nurse's assistant, learned about the new philosophy on neuro-renal, it brought a big smile to his face. "I said, 'This is what we need. We just needed to put a name to it.'"

A few years earlier, when Leo was 22, his father had died. "It was all very mysterious to me," he says. "I wish I had known half the things I know now. But there was no one who ever came to me and tried to take that pain away.

"When I got the chance to work at Missouri Baptist and had that first experience with working with someone who was in pain, and got to do something about it, I knew then I could never turn back. I used to work with cancer patients and I had to learn that for some of them, life really is short. Why make that time full of memories of pain, when you can try to throw some joy to them?"

Leo decided to create joy with music. "When patients are down, I sing little songs to them, or I do my own little Elvis impression, and it perks them up. Recently we had an older patient who wouldn't eat. Her daughter came to get me because she said I seemed to have a way with her mother. I sat down with the patient and said I would sing a little for her if she would take a few bites. She ate half her meal. That was pretty cool.

"I really enjoy getting a rapport going with the patient like that, and getting a comfort level with their family members. Nothing makes me feel better than when a family member tells me, 'Knowing that you're going to be here tonight will let me sleep with ease.'"

But for many neuro-renal patients, sleeping peacefully isn't easy. "We call them 'sundowners,'" Leo says. "When the sun goes down, some people who seem mentally clear and are easy to deal with during the day seem to lose their sense of place. They may become confused and agitated. They don't know where they are and they don't know who you are."

Sometimes the sundowners try to get out of bed. "Occasionally we put people in a chair and wheel them to the nurses' station for a while," Leo says. "We tell them it's so they can keep us company, but it's really so we can keep an eye on them so they don't fall."

One night Leo was taking vital signs from a patient who was in his 90s and near death. The patient was incoherent, agitated, and trying to pull out his IV. Leo tried to calm him down, but nothing was working. So he started singing softly. That didn't work either. Leo began to think he might have to get a doctor's order to restrain the man. He never liked having to do that.

Just then Olya Senchenkova, R.N., came into the room. As she and Leo considered what to do next, Olya said, "Did you know he used to be the conductor of a symphony orchestra?"

"Really?" Leo said. He had a long list of duties yet to complete, but he thought for a moment. "You know, I have my clarinet in my car."

"Go get it," she said. "I'll cover for you."

Leo had played clarinet in his college's marching band; his niece had been borrowing the clarinet and had just returned it. He assembled the instrument, then practiced for a minute or two. "I hadn't played in a year," Leo says. "I didn't want this master conductor to rip it out of my mouth."

Leo returned to the room. He played the first classical piece that came to mind, "Peter and the Wolf," and then the theme from *The Muppet Show*.

As the soft, mellow notes drifted through the room, something happened. The old man stopped thrashing. He closed his eyes and smiled. Lying on his back, he raised his arms and began to wave them back and forth. Perhaps, deep in his mind, he was standing in a great concert hall once again, wearing coat and tails, with a baton in his strong hands, leading *his* orchestra. After a few minutes the old man's arms dropped slowly to his sides and he slept quietly through the night.

It was the only night Leo took care of the conductor. Leo had the next few days off and when he returned to work, he learned that the man had died. The conductor's family said he was peaceful when he left them, and they were thankful for that.

LETTING WONDERFUL EMERGE

In May 2000, several months after introducing the FISH! Philosophy to neuro-renal, Shari Bommarito repeated her original teamwork survey. The turnaround, especially in the number of staff who *strongly* felt the presence of teamwork, was remarkable.

FiSH! TALES

	SEPTEMBER 1999	MAY 2000
FELT INDICATOR WAS	**TEAMWORK**	**TEAMWORK**
LACKING	25	10
PRESENT	45	15
STRONG	**30**	**75**
FELT INDICATOR WAS	**ATTITUDE**	**ATTITUDE**
LACKING	25	15
PRESENT	50	10
STRONG	**25**	**75**
FELT INDICATOR WAS	**COMMUNICATION**	**COMMUNICATION**
LACKING	15	20
PRESENT	52	15
STRONG	**33**	**65**
FELT INDICATOR WAS	**SUPPORT**	**SUPPORT**
LACKING	25	10
PRESENT	50	15
STRONG	**25**	**75**
FELT INDICATOR WAS	**SATISFACTION**	**SATISFACTION**
LACKING	25	15
PRESENT	50	10
STRONG	**25**	**75**
FELT INDICATOR WAS	**HAVE A SAY**	**HAVE A SAY**
LACKING	33	20
PRESENT	52	15
STRONG	**15**	**65**

"In the first survey, when I asked them what a team was, people said the names of sports teams, like the Rams or Cardinals," Shari says. "Now they said *their* teams—the Barracuda, the Angelfish.

"And instead of saying, 'I don't have time to help you,' people said, 'I'm busy right now, but I'll be there in a second. Can you wait?' That's what was missing. Those wonderful people were there all the time. They just didn't have time to be wonderful because they weren't working together.

"The nurses had stopped being nurses. All we did was say, 'This is why you came here. Have fun. Take a few minutes to be there for your patient. We will work as a team. We will get the job done together.'

"That's what Leo did. He had a list of tasks as long as anyone, but he took a few minutes to play the clarinet for a confused old man. He was able to do that because Olya watched his patients. They worked as a team.

"And instead of sitting in my office listening to people in the halls say, 'I need help!' now I got off my rear to go help them. I had to walk the talk, too."

SPREADING THE JOY

Word of what was happening on the neuro-renal floor spread throughout Missouri Baptist. "You'd get on the elevator with your fish on your badge and people would say, 'Hey, you're from the fish floor,'" Leo says.

The neuro-renal staff won Missouri Baptist's annual Quality Team Award, given to the team that did the most to improve patient care. As part of the award, the staff won $1,000. They gave half to the family of one of their patients for a Christmas present and used the rest for a Christmas party.

"Patients and relatives often told us they could see that what we were doing really helped patients," says Lois Wright, R.N., director of nursing services.

Soon other floors began asking for the FISH! Philosophy. "Our floor had a hard time with that," Shari says. "We kind of wanted it for ourselves. But then we said, 'How fishy is that?'" Soon they were sharing what they had discovered.

But when some operating room staff asked Shari to teach them about the philosophy, she hesitated. High stress, a staffing shortage, and resistance to change had fueled a deep sense of negativity there. Just as she had feared, during her presentation some people sat in the back and said things like, "Keep your fish. Give us the cash."

Such comments didn't stop others from trying to bring some positive energy to the OR. The staff created a bulletin board where you could recognize coworkers who went out of their way to help someone, and Nancy Hesselbach, R.N., director of surgical services, bought a talking fish to hang on the wall.

Then somebody stole the fish.

Upset, Nancy posted a note asking the kidnappers to return her fish or leave money to replace him. The kidnappers responded by leaving a message on Hesselbach's answering machine: "We have Billy. Do what we say or you'll never see him again." In the background, Billy was gurgling.

Nancy made up a flyer saying, "Please Return My Baby Billy," and offered a prize for information leading to the arrest and conviction of his kidnappers. His captors responded by dropping a can of tuna on her desk and a note saying this is what was to become of her beloved Billy.

"The staff were really into what was happening to Billy," Nancy says. "They wrote poems, songs, and epitaphs to Billy. We outlined the shape of a fish on our floor with masking tape and set it up like a crime scene with a 'Do Not Cross' police line. People were in stitches over this for weeks."

Before anyone realized it, the OR staff—including those most negative about the FISH! Philosophy—were having fun at work.

The "kidnappers" finally instructed Nancy to bring coffee and donuts to the next staff meeting. She complied, and later found a talking fish resembling Billy with duct tape over his mouth. "Billy's back and he'll never be the same. He's better than ever. Thanks for a successful campaign," read the accompanying note.

The OR later organized committees to explore ways to create a better workplace environment. "There are still people who want nothing to do with it, but others are trying to make a difference," says Shari. "They are making baby steps."

Missouri Baptist began to spread the FISH! Philosophy to other areas of the medical center. "Every hospital system in our state is having trouble recruiting nurses," explains Sheila Reed, a program development specialist at the Clinical Nursing Institute. "Instead of just trying to recruit, we need to retain our excellent staff. Money makes some difference, but the underlying reason most people like their jobs is due to other factors, such as their coworkers or the atmosphere."

As of summer 2001, Admitting was the latest area to introduce these principles. "The last time I walked down there, they had fish on the top of their computers," Shari says. "I said, 'You're right on target.' That's why we decorated our area with fish. Patients and visitors will ask about it and your staff are going to have to reaffirm it, and every time they talk about it, they're going to start walking it. You just have to keep cheering for them."

SWIMMING IN THE SAME DIRECTION

Back on neuro-renal, the work didn't change. It was still just as tiring, frustrating, and emotionally draining. What did change was the attitude the staff chose to bring to their work.

"We had a patient with renal failure who was with us for several weeks," Shari says. "Her family was nice but very demanding. At times it seemed like her husband expected more care and more time than any nurse could have given. The nurses worked hard to fulfill his high expectations and it didn't seem like it was ever really enough."

"We had been through a lot with this family and, yeah, they had frustrated all of us at some point, but they were frustrated too," Sharon Sanders says. "They were watching their loved one die and we had to realize where they were at."

On the day the woman was to be discharged, Shari Bommarito was working in her office when Hilda stuck her head in. "Come out here right now," Hilda said.

In the hall was the patient's husband. A group of nurses was gathered around him. He was holding a watercolor painting.

"I painted this years ago and it never sold," he said. "I'm not sure why." He held up the painting for the nurses. Swimming on the canvas were beautiful tropical fish of many colors.

"My painting is called *Harmony*," he said. "Like the fish in this painting, you are all different. You are different people and different colors and you come from different places . . . but you are all swimming in the same direction. You made a difference for my wife . . . and I would like you to have this painting."

Shari stood in the back of the crowd, stunned. "This is one of those moments you hold on to," she says. "Hilda and I are sobbing, and I look at these nurses and I'm thinking, 'Do you hear what he's saying to you? Do you realize what you've done? You made a difference! You didn't think it was enough, but it made a difference!'"

"A SIMPLE CHOICE"

As recognition for being the first floor at Missouri Baptist to introduce the FISH! Philosophy, the staff was awarded bright purple-and-blue jackets decorated with tropical fish. No other floor can wear them.

In the process, Shari realized something essential about the FISH! Philosophy. "When we started all this, I worshiped the guys at Pike Place Fish. They're wonderful. But they're no different than we are."

Pike Place Fish has fans known as the Yogurt Dudes, who come during their lunch hour just to watch the fishmongers work. "Leo took pictures of the staff, cut them out in the shape of a fish, and put them on a poster," Shari says. "Pretty soon patients wanted their picture on the poster too. We said, 'Oh my gosh, we have Yogurt Dudes!'

"Then I heard one of our nurses telling a graduate nurse she was training, 'You have to choose to be here and you have to *choose* whether you want to have a good day or not. It's a simple choice.'

"I walked by her a few minutes later and I told her, 'You are a fishmonger.'"

SMALL BITES

⋈ ROBBIE'S STORY ⋈

We heard this story from a blood transfusion service. Every week since birth, a four-year-old boy named Robbie needed all of his blood replaced. Every month Robbie's parents went to one of the service's seven locations and thanked every worker, volunteer, and donor for making it possible for their son to live. Many employees kept a picture of Robbie in their offices to remind them of who they were "being" while serving others. Is there something *you* can bring to work to remind *you* to "be there?"

⋈ TWO HUNDRED COOKIES ⋈

A friend named Harry stopped at a fast-food restaurant and placed an order that included a cookie. The server said, "And would you like a cookie with that today?" The next time Harry returned to the restaurant, he placed the same order, cookie included, with a different server. Again, the server politely asked, "Would you like a cookie with that?"

The third time Harry dealt with yet another server. This

time he was feeling a little mischievous. He placed his order, then added, "And I would like two hundred cookies." To which the server said, without a trace of irony, "I'll get that for you, sir. And would you like a cookie with that?"

Yes, the employees were told to say that. But were they really present when they did?

LOOKING FOR BLUSH

When an elderly woman came into an optical store looking for blush, it would have been easy for the store employee just to point her in the direction of the cosmetics store. But she took time off to walk her through the mall to the store, then out to her car. The elderly woman said just three words but they came straight from her heart: "God bless you."

SITTING WITH MOM

In December 2000, Steve's 84-year-old mom moved in with him and his wife. They took the family room with attached bathroom on the first floor and made it her home. "It has been delightful to be able to knock on the door and drop in," he says. "I haven't had this proximity to Mom since I was a kid."

The example set by the fish guys has helped Steve "be there" for his mother. At first he would knock on her door and go in and chat while standing. Something didn't feel quite right but it took a while to understand what was missing. Now he knocks, goes in, and sits on the couch. The act of sitting down helps him to be there and makes the visit more pleasant for both of them—

even if it is a short stay. Sitting not only sends a message to his mom but it also serves as a cue for him to be where he is.

Recently Steve noticed something his mother does to "be there" for him: "When I visit Mom, and she has the TV on, she picks up a pencil to push the remote and turn off the TV, something she can't do with her fingers. This gesture speaks volumes about how she values my visits. Why didn't I notice that before?"

✄ THANKS FOR MAKING A DIFFERENCE ✄

After John Christensen had given a speech, five or six people at a time came up to him to talk more about how they could bring more energy to their work. "I tried to listen to them all," he recalls. "One woman was so excited about all the things she was doing at work. I heard what she was saying and I said, 'That's lovely,' but I didn't really look her in the eye."

Two days later John remembered the encounter. She had given him her card. He immediately called her, apologized for not being present, and thanked her for everything she was doing to improve the lives of her coworkers. A few days later, he got a letter from her. "You called me at an incredible time," she wrote. "I thought I wasn't making a difference anymore. Now I know I do."

✄ WHAT IS LOVE? ✄

The other day Steve Lundin was sitting at his desk and daydreaming while looking at a picture of his daughter Melissa, her husband Paul, and their two darling children. "I am really proud of the way Missy and Paul are raising their children and Mia and Madeleine are thriving," Steve says. "I thought about all the love that is present in their home. When the word love came to mind I asked myself a question. 'What is love?' The answer followed quickly. 'Love, for a child, is being there.'"

✄ GOING DOG-FISHING ✄

Paul, a university dean, had by his own admission become a workaholic. But one day, hearing about how the fishmongers practice being present, he decided to be there for himself and those he loved. He visualized the most important person in his life, Joyce, and a dog walking on the shores of a lake.

That afternoon, to the amazement of his colleagues and his family, he left work on time for the first time in months. And that afternoon Paul and Joyce walked their dog along Lake Superior. The rest of the summer, he left work no later than 5 p.m. He and Joyce often walked—and he and his dog often went dog-fishing (retrieving tennis balls from the lake).

✄ A VALUABLE SERVICE ✄

We expect the people who serve us in stores and restaurants to be there for us. *But are we there for them?* Our colleague Carr Hagerman was talking on his cell phone as a clerk rang up his purchases. Suddenly, he said into the cell phone, "I need to hang up now so I can be with the clerk."

The clerk looked into Carr's eyes. "Thank you," she said. "You just made me valuable."

Section Four–CHOOSE YOUR ATTITUDE

*The attitude you have right now is the one you are choosing.
Is it the one you want?*

From our very first visit to Pike Place Fish, we were struck by the number of conversations about choice. The fish guys are always talking about their choice to be at work and their choice to have a good day. I can only speculate about where the idea emerged. A few of the guys are 12-steppers like me, and choice is certainly a part of that process. "Choose your attitude" provides a solid base for this marvelous business culture.

THE SNAKE STORY

I first heard the following story at a Stephen Covey seminar in 1985. I know the story has been around longer than that, but it was the first time I heard it.

Three high school graduates, two men and a woman, were walking in the Arizona desert when a rattlesnake, coiled in the dark, bit the woman. The two guys took off after the snake and eventually caught it and brought it back. Meanwhile the woman, left to deal with the venom, nearly died.

The point is that at one time or another, life bites us all. The choice is the same in each case. We can chase the snakes in our lives or deal with the poison.

In the story that follows, a roofing company demonstrates in many ways the power of choice. I especially love their willingness to enter into what can be difficult conversations. As a result they are proving the truth of the following statement:

> The greatest discovery of my generation is that a human being can alter his life by altering his attitude.
>
> —William James (1842–1910)

Let It Rain:
Tile Technology Roofing Company

It's warm inside the truck, and the coffee's hot, but every squeak of the windshield wipers betrays the morning's cold reality. Rain is pouring from the gray, mountain-lined skies of Tacoma, and it's just a few degrees from turning into snow.

There's a Catch-22 in roofing: You wear rain gear to stay dry, but lifting thousands of pounds of tile shingles all day makes you sweat, and then you're freezing *and* wet 20 feet in the air.

Russ Vieselmeyer would rather be sitting in front of a blazing fire thinking about snowboarding, but he and his crew from Tile Technology Roofing Company have a job to finish. When they put the last piece of tile in place later today, rain won't penetrate this family's home for several decades.

As Russ piles out of the truck, he knows he has a choice today. He gives one of his crew a high-five and as the freezing drops sting his face he stares up into the heavens and laughs.

"Is that all you got?" he yells. "Bring it on!"

CHOOSING TO BE GREAT

Lives are made up of millions of choices. Some are made for you but it's the choices you make that count the most.

Doug Vieselmeyer, Russ's older brother, was seven when his parents divorced. Then, his mother, Connie, was stricken with lupus, which can cause the immune system to attack healthy tissues and organs. She was 6′ 1″ and strong, but the disease—which was initially misdiagnosed—left her so weak she couldn't even open baby food jars for Doug's younger siblings. "I would run over and ask the neighbor lady to do it," Doug recalls.

Lupus often comes and goes without warning. Sometimes Connie Vieselmeyer spent long stretches where she was nearly bedridden. Sometimes the disease went into remission. "She went back to college, finished her teaching degree, and taught third grade for a few years," Doug says. "Then the lupus came back."

While some days were better than others, "she still found joy in every day of her life. There was always love in our house. If she could no longer do something physically, she focused on what she *could* do. When all she could do was sit, she made gifts for people, because she couldn't afford to buy them."

Because of his mother's illness, Doug had to grow up quickly. "I kind of missed my childhood, parts of it anyway," he explains. "We were on welfare, and kids will humiliate you any way they can when they get something on you. Between growing so fast [Doug is 6′ 10″ today], wearing pants that were too short, and having other kids see me paying at the grocery store with food stamps, I decided to get a job."

Doug was only 13, but he told the manager of a shoe store that he was 16. He sold enough Earth Shoes to become the store's leading salesperson and paid for his family's food and rent. The height that helped him get his first job later helped him earn a college basketball scholarship. He graduated with a degree in marketing and business administration, and took a job as an underwriter with an insurance company.

To earn extra money on weekends, he roofed with his friend Glen Paine. Like Doug, Glen was raised by a single mother on welfare, and had started working when he was 13. He was competitive, driven to succeed, and focused on how to roof faster, longer, harder, and better.

Doug, on the other hand, had no great love for roofing. "There's nothing pretty about it," he says. "It's hard on you and it's dangerous." But everybody needed a roof, the job paid well—and Doug did not envision spending the rest of his life with his full-time employer. "I saw people who had spent 20, 25, 30 years forced into early retirement," he says. "I wasn't going to dedicate my life to climbing the corporate ladder just to have it pulled out from underneath me someday."

Doug quit his underwriting job, and he and Glen decided to start a roofing company. "Glen already had the experience, but I picked roofing for an odd reason," Doug says. "I figured an average guy like me might have a chance at being great at it."

Doug talked his mother into putting up her home as security for a contractor's license. Glen supplied a few tools and a

20-year-old flatbed pickup painted with black primer. In November 1987, Tile Technology Roofing Company opened in Tacoma, Washington.

REDEFINING SUCCESS

Tile Tech was founded on a simple principle: "Do what you're going to do when you say you're going to do it."

"At the time, nobody in the roofing industry seemed to follow through with what they said they were going to do," Doug explains. "If you said, 'I'll be there on Wednesday,' that meant anywhere between Wednesday and the following Monday. It drove me crazy. Glen and I thought, 'If you just do what you say you're gonna do, I don't see how you could lose.'"

For its first five years, Tile Tech's only form of advertising was to do a good job. "We didn't have a number in the phone book, we had zero advertising, no names or phone numbers on our vehicles," Glen says. "We just kept our word and followed through."

In Tile Tech's first year, it made $750,000 in revenues and $100,000 in pretax profit. By 1999, annual revenues exceeded $10 million, Tile Tech employed 100 people, and it was developing a strong regional reputation for its roofs on homes, hotels, hospitals, apartments, and government buildings. Two highly respected professionals, Bob Deaton and Don Vose, also had joined the Tile Tech ownership team.

Poised for growth, Tile Tech sank hundreds of thousands of dollars into equipment needed to win larger roofing contracts.

But when the company, along with its competitors, encountered a shortage of experienced roofers, it realized that long-term relationships with its employees were the key to its success.

Roofing was not a business built on lasting relationships. Most companies gave its new roofers minimal training, made them pay for their own tools, and set them to work with little or no supervision. Not surprisingly, many young roofers lived from paycheck to paycheck and drifted from company to company. Most companies also paid roofers by each piece they completed, which encouraged speed over quality, especially among inexperienced workers.

"There are some terrible recent roof jobs out there," a columnist wrote in the *Seattle Times*. "These are not roofs installed by the Fly-By-Night Roofing Co., the guys who offer that exclusive 'until-your-check-has-cleared-or-you-can't-see-my-taillights' warranty. These are roofs installed by companies with good reputations."

Tile Tech decided to do things differently. It reorganized its roofing teams into a mixture of salaried, hourly, and piece-work employees. The salaried supervisors made sure the team did a quality job and taught the new roofers, who were paid by the hour. Only experienced roofers, who knew how to do the job right *and* fast, were paid by the piece. Tile Tech also created a new career ladder for its roofers that tied their income to training, performance, and leadership skills.

"Rather than being in denial about this endemic problem," the *Seattle Times* columnist later wrote, Tile Tech has "stepped up and done something to change it. Bravo."

CHOOSING A LEGACY

Tile Tech was just as interested in helping its employees develop skills beyond the workplace. Roofing is a hard job and it often attracts people with hard lives. "Some of our guys have grown up in difficult family situations," Doug explains. "Many of them are afraid to show any kind of emotion. You walk up to greet them and I don't know if they've ever been hugged before. Some have had problems with alcohol."

As Tile Tech become successful, Doug, by his own admission, went "a little crazy, I bought some nice toys, house, car—stuff. But I realized that wasn't what happiness really was. I remembered as a kid, being with my family, at school and church—that was where I found happiness.

"As we expanded, I wanted to learn how to treat people properly and encourage them to grow." Doug began investing in himself, reading books and attending seminars, and he discovered a world of wisdom that was open to anyone with the desire to seek it. "It raised my awareness about a lot of things. Glen and I saw that our company wasn't roofs or assets; it was people. We saw that maybe we could help other people raise their awareness. Not trying to change anyone, just letting them know that they had choices in their lives."

Tile Tech became active in community work. When the company heard about an elderly woman whose roof was so rotten that parts of it would blow off in strong winds, it helped replace it and cleaned up her yard. Tile Tech did not forget about its own community either. The company sponsored contests that invited employees to volunteer in their communities, avoid alcohol and chemical dependency, be safe at work, pursue personal goals—"things as simple as bringing flowers to your wife or girlfriend once in a while," Doug says. "If employees want to talk about it, we've gone down about every path there is—addiction, relationships, marriage, children."

With every roof it installs, Tile Tech leaves a legacy. "But the big one is the legacy we're leaving for our children," says Doug.

SPEAKING THEIR LANGUAGE

Soon the walls of Tile Tech were covered with motivational quotes and pictures of employee accomplishments—not the kind of decor that most roofing companies chose. Still, something was missing. "It was like the gears weren't quite in sync," Doug says. "I'd say 20 percent of the employees were really into what we were trying to accomplish, but the other 80 were on the fence."

Then the management team heard a talk about the World Famous Pike Place Fish market. They had all visited the market—Seattle was not far away—and thought it seemed like a great place to work, but they didn't know why. The speaker explained that every day, every moment, each of the fishmongers took personal responsibility for choosing the actions and attitudes they brought to work.

Tile Tech's leaders immediately saw how much the fishmongers had in common with their roofing crews—mostly young men doing a job few others wanted to do. Yet the fish-mongers magically remade their environment through the power of their attitudes.

"It absolutely hit home with us," Bob Deaton explains. "Sometimes we deal with rain, wind, or snow. Sometimes it's too cold or too hot. Are you going to be upset every single day?"

When Bob told his roofers about the fishmongers, they walked out of the office on a cloud. "They could not wait to get back to work," he said. "Suddenly we had words for what we were trying to do."

When Russ Vieselmeyer saw the fishmongers in action, he thought, "They're talkin' right to me."

For employees like Brian Marchel, it was an invitation he had been waiting for. "I've always had a lifelong dream of being a positive person. As a kid, I had kind of a negative step-father," he says. "I stood up to him one day and I told him, 'I'm tired of you focusing on what I don't do, and you never say anything good about what I do.'"

Brian posted the words "Choose Your Attitude" on his front door. "As I walk out, I choose my attitude right then and there," he says. "Sometimes I don't wake up until I get about halfway to work, but then it kicks in."

CREATING AWARENESS

But Tile Tech's employees soon learned that what seems obvious is less easy to put into practice every day. At an early meeting to discuss how to transform their work, a woman announced, "You *can't* choose a @#$&%!! good attitude *every* day!"

Bob Deaton, who was leading the session, had to give her points for honesty. "There's truth in that," he told the rest of the employees. "But you do choose *some* type of attitude every day."

Bob began sharing strategies. "I read that to create a new habit you have to do something for 21 straight days," he told employees. "It's easy to say you're going to do it, but after a couple of days, you're right back to your old habits. To help me remember every day, I started putting a note next to my alarm radio: 'Choose an Attitude.'"

He also told employees to close their eyes. "If you were being promoted and you were going to hire someone to do your job, picture the perfect employee," he said. "What time would they come in? How would they be prepared? How would they talk about people? How would they perform their job?

"Now open your eyes and be that person. Because if you're that, you're awesome."

Throughout Tile Tech, people started to change their days through the power of choice. "Now when I get in the car in the morning, I do a quick assessment of how my day is going to go," says office manager Lisa Franklin. "I ask myself, 'Why I am there? What am I doing it for? What's important to me?'

"Because sometimes you may be having your first cup of coffee, and chatting with someone. If you're not ready and your brain is not on, you might get caught off guard. Your response might not be the best or might not be taken well."

And good attitudes spread quickly. "I started dispatching the guys to their jobs in the mornings," Bob says. "Before, I would have dreaded that assignment. There would be 60 to 70 roofers in here, most of 'em red-faced—and more cuss words than you can imagine. Now everybody comes in, pats each other on the back, says good morning. It's fun to come in. It's like meeting with your friends."

SHARING YOURSELF

Tile Tech's employees also learned that while a good attitude may be great, you need to share it with others. "Before, you'd come to work early, with your game face on, and you'd go right into your office and start working," Bob explains. "You wouldn't even pay attention to other people, maybe say 'Hey' once in a while."

No one at Tile Tech exemplified that culture more than Bob Deaton. "I'd be sitting at my desk, working on a bid, and someone would come up to me with a question or needing something," he recalls. "In the past I would say, 'Not now! I'm in the middle of something!' I basically blew them off without realizing it; I would not even remember they were there."

When Bob saw how the employees of Pike Place Fish work hard to be there for the people they serve, a light came on in his head. "I realized how wrong I was. I had to apologize to a lot of people. I realized it doesn't take much extra time to say good morning to people. I saw how much it means to walk over to new employees, shake their hand, and say, 'Welcome. How are you doing?'"

"Bob has really changed," says Heidi McCaig, human resources director. "He was crabby. But now he makes time for others and he's a good coach."

"This morning I was talking with one of our employees about the fact that he is becoming so focused on his work that he's walking past people without acknowledging them, and being in a hurry with folks," Bob says. "I told him, 'You have the Bob Deaton syndrome. You're being like I was.'

"He sat back, thought for a moment, and said, 'Wow, that really hits home, because I know how I felt about you. I was afraid to come near you. I'm gonna take more time for people.'"

THE SHREWSBERRY GREETING

Mornings at Tile Tech, which has its offices located in a remodeled rambler home with a swimming pool in the back, begins with coffee and the Ray Shrewsberry greeting. "I'm an upbeat guy, and roofers, you know, can be kind of gruff and stern," Ray, a quality control supervisor, explains. "So if I saw someone who wasn't as happy as I thought they should be, I'd yell out their full name, like 'Good morning, Bob Deaton!'"

"Every day this guy would walk past me and say, 'Good morning, Bob Deaton!' It brought a smile to my face every day," Bob says. "So we thought we should all try it. It was amazing how many employees there are whose full names you don't know, so it really helped us to learn them."

The people of Tile Tech are just as serious as they ever were about doing their work; they've just found a way to do it in a lighthearted way. "We have a little stuffed fish, and one of our guys, who has tattoos, pierced the fish's ear and gave him a tattoo," says Tim O'Brien, installation coordinator. "The other day, I had two phones going. One of my coworkers walked into my office, set the fish on my desk, and didn't say anything.

"She answered phones all the time, so she knew how many calls I was getting that day. It just made my day for her to do that. It was a little thing she did that made me feel better and got me through that time."

There's a more lighthearted approach among the roofing crews too. "We don't shoot staples at each other with the fastening guns anymore," says Brian. "Mostly we play through conversation, teasing each other and mentally picking each other up."

Sometimes Doug shows up at the job site with motorized scooters. "It doesn't have a darn thing to do with roofing," he explains. "But you should see these guys' faces when we take a break and have races."

LEARNING NEW TRICKS

Dwight Lambert is in his early 50s. His hair began heading north years ago, and his face is etched with years of hard weather and harder work. You wouldn't figure Dwight to be a

Britney Spears fan, yet there he is, tapping his toes to a Britney tune with a little girl outside her home before he climbs back on her parents' roof.

Dwight used to be known around Tile Tech as "the grouchy old guy," and as he admits, "I guess maybe I had reasons to be grouchy."

Dwight's parents divorced as he was about to become a teenager. His mother remarried, but "I figured my stepfather married her for her and not for me, and that was my attitude," he says. "I just kind of took the bull by the horns and did my own life."

He quit school after his sophomore year and went to work. He was a barber for a time, then worked steel, but whatever he did, he strove to be the best he could be. "My dad told me, 'If all you're gonna do is shovel horse manure, just be the best horse-manure shoveler you can be,' and I've done that all my life."

Dwight began roofing when he was in his mid-30s, an age when many roofers start looking for work that is easier on the body. But he worked smart and he excelled. He didn't even mind bad weather, he says, "because it separates the men from the boys."

It never occurred to him that he could enjoy his work, or enjoy the people he worked with. "For 17 years it was just me and the world. I went out and did my own thing. If you gave me a job, I didn't ask questions. I did it right and I got paid for it."

Sometimes, when working with others who didn't measure up to his exacting standards and exhausting pace, Dwight barked at them. "I guess starting out at an early age, having to think for myself all the time, I was too serious," he says. "Big things I can handle, but little things bother me, waste of time, petty crap. It really bothers me."

One day he was working with his sons and became upset with one of them. "I stomped over to him—we weren't wearing any safety equipment—and I slipped on a loose shingle. I lost my balance and fell feet first." On the way down he hit a $4'' \times 12''$ beam. "I broke my foot and had three screws put in it. I was down for nine months.

"It was one of those things that shouldn't have upset me, and maybe if I had taken an anger management class or something, it wouldn't have, but back then it was like, 'You don't like it? I don't care.'"

Dwight came to work for Tile Tech a few years ago, but he stayed less than a week. "Dwight was extremely dependable and he knew how to do the job," says Doug. "But he turned heads right away with 'This is the way I've always done it and you guys should be doing it my way.'"

Dwight later came back to Tile Tech, but this time he was introduced to how the fishmongers approach their work. "I thought it was silly at first," he says. "But I started to think about how it relates to real life. It brought me an awareness that life can be easier.

"I'm a product of my environment. I've never been in an environment where anyone really gives a damn, other than, 'Are you done? Here's the next one.' They say you can't teach an old dog new tricks. Well, maybe I'm the example that you can. Like I said, it wasn't that I didn't want to; I was just never in that position where anybody could slow me down enough to show me. But I think I was always looking for that. And now I am that."

Make no mistake, Dwight is intensely serious about his work, and he's not afraid to tell you how they *used* to do it. "Old school," the young guys call it. But more and more he's there for his young crew when they need him, sharing the experience he's gathered over the years. He's trying to have more fun at lunchtime. He wears safety equipment. He taps his toes to Britney Spears.

"Sometimes you gotta bark to get some people's attention; then again, if you learn other ways, it isn't necessary," he says. "You can have fun and get as much done and not be all upset at the end of the day.

"Life doesn't have to be that complicated. Twenty years ago, if someone cut in front of me on the highway, I'd holler and give hand motions. Now I just kind of chuckle, 'What's the hurry?' One more car ahead of me isn't gonna make any difference in my day."

Because now there are more important things to think about, like grandchildren. "I've got eight of 'em," Dwight says. "My oldest son's girlfriend has two sons. The oldest one, Andrew, said to me, 'Is it all right if I call you Grandpa Dwight?'

"It brought tears to my eyes. He doesn't have a grandpa. I said to him, 'I'd like it if you called me Grandpa Dwight.'"

Last spring, his wife, Kathy, underwent emergency surgery to repair a bleeding aneurysm. "I just about lost the most important person in my life," he says. "So me coming to work and getting upset . . . hey, no big deal."

STAYING SAFE FOR OTHERS

According to the Department of Labor and Industries, roofing is one of the most dangerous occupations.

When Doug applied for Tile Tech's roofing license in 1987, he says, "the state didn't say boo about safety. I didn't know what safety was, I didn't know you needed it, and then we found out the hard way. The state started enforcing and we got some violations."

Today Tile Tech has a safety committee, elected by its employees, that conducts a comprehensive training program with the Department of Labor and Industries. On angled roofs, employees wear full-body harnesses anchored to the truss.

Yet the decision to practice safety is ultimately an individual choice. "My philosophy has always been: 'If you don't respect yourself to work safely today, call me,'" Doug says. "'There won't be any penalty, you can go home today.'"

Tile Tech borrowed a technique from Pike Place Fish to increase safety awareness. "When one of the fish guys yells out an order, all the other fishmongers repeat it," Russ says. "Before we step on a roof, we walk around the job site. As we call out safety steps and possible hazards, the guys repeat it in cadence. When we do that, we know the guys have heard it. There's awareness."

And they have fun with it. A small swale prompts a cry of

"Thirty-foot ditch! Thirty-foot ditch! Thirty-foot ditch!" If someone is about to toss a piece of broken tile to the ground, he shouts, "Headache!" and the rest of the crew respond in turn, "Headache! Headache!"

Safety coordinator Steve Wallace travels from site to site, checking to make sure Tile Tech crews practice safety, "but I try to catch them doing positive things and praise them for it."

Tile Tech reminds its employees that safety isn't about protecting yourself from something. It's about protecting yourself *for* something. "We have had family nights where we invite spouses to learn more about our philosophies," Doug says. "I explain that I don't ever want to have to knock on their doors and tell them that their husband or son is not going to come home anymore. By using love, we've been able to get through to our people. Now they've caught onto it and it's become their idea."

In 1999, Tile Tech recorded 42 injuries. In 2000, it had 27. Through July 2001, the company had just 5 injuries, putting it on pace to finish with fewer than 10 for the year.

"SOMETHING'S DIFFERENT ABOUT YOU GUYS"

"In the past people would look out their windows and wonder what we were doing," Bob says. "[Our] mentality was: 'Leave us alone! We know what we're doing. You'll see the job when it's done.'"

Today Tile Tech has completely reversed that approach. If customers are interested, its roofing team leaders come down and ask if they have questions. "Instead of looking at it as another roof, we try to remember that it's their dream. We try to make them part of it. We invite them, if they want, to pound a nail in the roof. Heck, when home builders pour the concrete slab, they should invite customers to have their kids put in their initials. People remember things like that. They'll tell friends, 'I helped put on that roof,' and they'll never forget you for that."

When you are focused on another person, and not just yourself, little details take on greater importance. A customer once wrote a glowing testimonial to Tile Tech; his roof looked great, but what really caught his eye was watching one of the crew take the time to remove small pieces of the old roof from the flower garden.

"Before, the guys used to think it didn't matter how [they] acted or what [they] said or did, as long as the job got done," Bob says. "Now they realize how their attitude has a huge impact on the way people perceive our company."

"It's about being considerate," Russ says. "Some companies only clean up the site when the job is done. We clean up every night."

One day, after an exhausting 12-hour day on a roof, one of the guys climbed down and offered to play catch with the customer's son. "They threw the ball around for a while," recalls Brian. "It just totally astonished the customer and made his day."

Making someone's day doesn't end when the roof is on. "I used to call every customer when we were done with the job,"

Doug says. "I'd say, 'This is the owner of Tile Tech and I'd like to know how we did. I want to know the good and the bad.' This blew people away. They would say, 'You gotta be kidding me! Nobody does this anymore!'"

Today Tile Tech goes a step further. "In roofing, it's what you *don't* see that matters," explains Glen. "I bring a digital camera, climb on the roof, and take pictures of the job, then I go over the job with the client.

"I met with an older lady the other day. Her first question was, 'Did you guys leave garbage in my gutters?' I said, 'That's the first picture I took. Look at how clean your gutters are.' She couldn't climb up on her roof to check, and that was a huge thing to her."

There was a time when Tile Tech's customers, like those of most roofing companies, paid reluctantly. "Today that's never an issue," Glen says. "They look forward to paying their bill."

"I don't know what it is about you guys," a customer said after Dwight Lambert's crew had finished her roof. "But something's different. You've brought a new face to the construction industry."

COACHING THE VISION

At a company meeting in May 2000, Tile Tech added two words to its official name; the company is now known as *World Famous* Tile Technology Roofing.

But to become world famous, Doug cautioned, they would have to help each other. They would have to coach each other.

"Coaching is very much a burden," he told everyone. "You can't walk by a problem. When you see something that's not right, when you see broken tiles on a roof, or a truck tire that's low, don't just walk by it.

"And you won't let it go if you take ownership. It's your vision. Don't think that it's just my vision or Glen's or Bob's or Don's. This is for everybody. It's like a relationship. How's it going to work if one person is the boss all the time? It doesn't work, does it? So when we accept the invitation into our vision, we accept two responsibilities. One is to coach and the other is to be coachable."

Asking Tile Tech's employees to coach the owners was not easy. "I think our biggest battles have been giving people confidence that we will respect their coaching," Doug says. "That's not natural in corporate America. People have been programmed to think the owner is not going to listen to them."

Bob calls it "pigeon management. You dump all over people, fly away, wait for 'em to make a mistake, and come back and dump on 'em again.

"When I started in this business 21 years ago, you kept your mouth shut, the boss yelled at you, and you worked. That's just how I was taught. I thought as long as you showed up earlier than anyone else and outworked them, that was a good manager."

But Bob learned it doesn't matter who the words come from; all that matters are the words being spoken. "I was having a loud conversation by the front desk and one of the employees asked if I could go somewhere else because one of the people answering the phones couldn't hear. I started to say, 'Are you trying to tell me what to do?' Then I stopped and asked myself if she was right. Yes, she was."

"I accepted some coaching from our office manager yesterday, and it was so helpful," Don Vose says. "That's a great thing when your employees have the confidence to come to ownership and say, 'I think you're doing something wrong.' And it's even better when ownership says, 'You're right.'"

Glen handled the challenge by being honest with his feelings. "Doug is comfortable in the lead role. I was the guy behind the scenes, but I was definitely in control there."

So when it came time to accept coaching from others, Glen said, "I'm new at this. Don't expect me to be perfect the first time, or the second or the third. I want to be a great listener, a great team player, and to be coachable—but I'm not there yet, so bear with me. So bring the coaching on. I'm gonna grit my teeth and hope I don't say the wrong thing.

"I never used to be a good listener. I didn't look into people's eyes. But I am getting better, especially with my wife and two-year-old daughter. I think the guys see a difference in me too. I used to have kind of a chip on my shoulder, where I didn't let people get too close to me. Now they see me changing, and it changes the way they go out the door."

GOING INTO THE POND

The leadership of Tile Tech once heard the poet David Whyte talk about *Beowulf*, the great epic in which the hero decides he must descend into a lake to battle a swamp-dwelling monster. That lake, Whyte says, is inside each of us. Our fear of going into that lake, into the difficult conversations it represents, can be so overwhelming that we would rather live unhappily than to descend into the lake to find the happiness, honesty, and healed relationships that may await us there.

"When you work closely with people every day, it's easy to become upset with someone or upset others," Bob says. "Those incidents can turn into grudges, and go on and on until you can't even remember the minor incident that happened."

That's why Tile Tech created the Pond. The Pond is a room in the back of the office. Inside is a small plastic swimming pool with sand and an umbrella, a few posters, and two chairs.

"The Pond is for when you need to have a conversation with someone," Bob says. "Maybe someone stepped on your toes, or you think they're not listening to you, or they're doing something that's not consistent with our vision of being world famous. You have the right to ask any person, regardless of their rank in the company, to go to the Pond. There you are on equal ground, and you can say what's on your mind: 'This is what you said or did, and this is how it made me feel.'"

There are no rules in the Pond, except to be respectful. You can be there for 15 minutes or two hours, whatever it takes. "You must be willing to speak your truth, and if you are judgmental or have a hidden agenda, or beat around the bush, the Pond doesn't work," Doug says. "You have to let go of your ego and your sense of righteousness; otherwise you are undermining the power of the Pond."

"Sometimes couples, friends, family members will have disagreements and they give up. They stop talking," Lisa says. "In the Pond we have to finish. In some situations it may be that we agree to disagree but we reach a conclusion."

"When there's a problem, you have to bring closure to it, because until you have closure you cannot go back to creating world famous," Bob says. "It's also important if you're a manager and an employee takes you to the Pond, to not strike back negatively. Because you'll have ruined them and they will never do it again."

Not everyone is comfortable with the Pond, but many have used it. Tile Tech's owners have all been taken to the Pond, and they have taken people there. Damaged relationships have been healed, and new relationships created. Conversations in the Pond have led people to make changes that helped them earn promotions; they also led an employee to leave Tile Tech because he was not comfortable with its direction. Some employees say the lessons of the Pond have helped them to communicate more effectively with their spouses and children.

"It's like going onstage," says Lisa, who was a professional singer before joining Tile Tech. "You pour your heart and soul into your song, to the people who are listening. They might clap and they might boo. You don't know what's going to happen, but you have to put it out there.

"Once you do it, it feels so good. I have yet to be in a position where I've poured out my heart and not gotten a good response. It may not be a fun response, but it's a response that in the end makes me feel better."

"Today we have cell phones and pagers—you name it—but we don't really communicate with the people in our lives," Doug says. "The Pond is a private time, almost a sacred time. It's your time to connect with another person. And we are starting to connect with each other."

TILE TECH'S SECRET

One of Tile Tech's employees had been having some personal problems, so Doug, a close friend, invited him to church. "About halfway through the sermon, he leans over and says, 'Did you tell the preacher what to say today? Because he's speakin' right to me.'

"I just chuckled. We think that we're the only one who's going through this problem, and really we're not. We all share common problems."

And common dreams. "Roofers have feelings and questions and emotions. They want to be part of a great enterprise where they matter and their opinion matters," Glen says. "Once we started using their opinions we became a better company."

That's why Tile Tech puts as much as $250,000 into employee development a year. "Trust me, the return has been tenfold that," Doug says.

"It's not real common in our industry to do that, and while most people really appreciate it, in some cases they don't. That's OK. It has to be unconditional. We take our gambles, but it can be a transient industry, and we invest a lot of time and money into people who turn away. But all it takes is a few people to make it work. They're like seeds; they will grow and touch others.

"Taking responsibility for your attitude and working with others and 'growing' other people, that's a big burden. If you come to our company, you are expected to grow other people once you've grown yourself. We have the opportunity to lift each other up, through all the peaks and valleys, and that's how we're going to get where we want to go together.

"At our Christmas party last year, Glenn Robb, our sales manager, came up to me and said, 'I figured out your secret.' I looked at him kind of funny and he goes, 'You guys figured out how to use love in your business.'

"I just winked at him and left it at that. I didn't have to say anything. I'd known for years what it was."

SMALL BITES

"MOMMY, IT'S RAINING!"

One of our favorite stories is of a six-year-old British girl whose mother introduced her to the FISH! Philosophy. A week later the little girl was getting ready for school on a dreary day. As she was about to leave for the bus stop she said, "Mommy, it's raining outside, but I'm going to have a FISH! day." The principle of choosing your attitude is clearly within the reach of a six-year-old.

WHAT DO YOU OWN?

A parable: Three neighbors were talking when the subject of possessions came up. "I own a huge mansion!" one proudly proclaimed. "I own a successful farm!" said the second. "I have optimism," the third said quietly. His two neighbors laughed at him, for what good is a possession that cannot be seen or touched?

That night a huge storm struck. The storm destroyed the first neighbor's house. "What am I to do?" he cried. The storm ruined the second neighbor's crops. "What will I do?" he lamented. The storm also destroyed the third neighbor's home and farm. "Hmmm, what should I do first?" he asked himself and then he began doing it. He rebuilt his home and replanted his crops.

His neighbors had been sitting this entire time, feeling sorry for themselves. But they watched their neighbor rebuild and they decided to ask him his secret. "It is no secret," the man said. "The only thing I own is what I think." The two neighbors suddenly understood, and with the third neighbor's help, they rebuilt too.

From then on, whenever they met, they did not talk about possessions. They talked about their blessings, and they shared them, for what sense does it make to hold on to something you do not own?

WITH ARMS WIDE OPEN

We recently read about a little boy with a rare digestive disorder. He spent much of his time in the hospital, with needles in his arms. When a doctor or nurse approached him, he knew it was because they were probably going to have to put another needle in his arm. But instead of crying, he smiled and held out his arms for them.

Life can sometimes be painful when you greet it with arms extended. But there is no other way to fully embrace life.

✂ **"YOU KNOW THAT GUY BEAR?"** ✂

With his gravelly voice, husky build, and face full of hair, Bear is one of the most recognizable fishmongers. Bear understands the power of choice. "You gotta choose where you're gonna be as soon as you get out of the bed," he says. "I do consciously make that choice every day."

One day we got a call from a gravelly-voiced employee at an automobile manufacturing plant. "You know that guy Bear—the guy who looks like he could kick your butt?" he growled amiably. "That's me." But now, every morning before the auto worker came to work, he said, he looked in the mirror and *chose* who he was going to be that day. "I've been coming to work here for 20 years, and if I can do it, so can these young guys."

✂ **SAVING A RELATIONSHIP** ✂

A woman at a seminar wanted to share her story with us. She told of a marriage on the rocks and growing bitterness between two people who had once felt close. With nothing to lose, she chose to bring the FISH! Philosophy into her fading relationship with her husband. One day she would try to make his day. The next she tried to create lighthearted experiences. When she started listening deeply to him, the effect was powerful; neither one of them had been there for the other for some time. He began to reciprocate.

We followed up with the woman months later. She and

her husband had still decided to follow through with the divorce. We were surprised, for we had somehow expected a fairy-tale ending. But life does not always proceed according to plan. The woman had still chosen to make a difference, and because of her action, all of the anger was gone. Now, instead of two warring adults going to battle, they were two caring adults who had decided to go their separate ways. The lessons of the fish market had not saved a marriage, but they had saved a friendship.

✂ EVEN ON TUESDAYS ✂

After a large school district adopted the lessons of the fish market to help bring more passion to its work, a skeptical school board member happened to be in Seattle during the week. He visited Pike Place Fish, and he discovered all the energy and wholeheartedness he had thought was not possible. "I thought this was a weekend thing," he said. "I didn't expect this to be real on a Tuesday afternoon." Every new day requires a new choice: Who are you going to be today?

✂ A MONKEY ON YOUR BACK ✂

Did you sleep late? Was getting the kids to school a battle? Was traffic horrible? At one hospital, if you show up in a less-than-happy mood, you are invited to wear a stuffed monkey on your back. It's a way of acknowledging the state of mind that's weighing you down—and you cannot change what you are thinking until you become aware of it.

ROCKS, SKIS, AND HOPE

It was 1978, and a young college professor felt his life was falling apart. He was recently divorced, barely had a dime to his name, and his former wife had moved away from Idaho with their sons. All he had were some rocks he and his sons had collected on the day before they left. Somehow they gave him a little hope.

One day the young professor's father bought him some skis, poles, boots, and a lift ticket. The young man fell down the hill all morning. At one point some of his students, who were skiing with him, circled around him. "Get up!" they said. Something welled up inside him; it felt like hope. He got up and skied down the hill for the first time. He skied all day. It was one of the most exhilarating days of his life. On the last run, knowing that the day was ending and he would be working the next day, he said out loud, "I work like I ski!" He wrote those words on a sign and put it in his office.

His sons soon returned to Idaho, and with their father, they enjoyed a life of skiing together. The young professor tried to pay his father back for the skis, but his father refused. "Just pass it on," he said. The professor, who is now a university dean, tries to pass it on every chance he gets.

The rocks are still sitting in a bowl on his desk, and they always will be.

Section Five-LET'S GO FISH!NG

FISH! for 12 weeks and discover the richer and more rewarding life that is just a few choices away.

This section is designed for those who wish to bring the FISH! Philosophy into their lives and would like a few ideas. Included are 12 weeks' worth of activities. Some of these have been field-tested with unsuspecting students and seminar participants, but most are presented here for the first time.

As you work through these exercises, remember that Full Life = Work Life + The Rest of Life. It may seem like a silly reminder. Of course life at work is part of a full life. Yet many of us find ourselves devaluing our work life when we treat it as something we must pass through on the way to the rest of life. For instance:

🐼 Are there things at work you take for granted but without these things your life would have less abundance?

🐼 Are there times you are doing one thing and already thinking about the next, thereby losing all that the present moment has to offer?

✖ Are there people who serve you every day whom you don't really see and without whom much of what you take for granted would come to a halt?

Now it is time to claim the one work life that is yours to live fully. OK, it may take more than 12 weeks—but the following exercises are a start.

Week One: FISH! Swim Best in a Sea of Gratitude

My daughter Melanie participated in the Semester at Sea program during her junior year at Santa Clara University. The SS *Universe Explorer* sailed from Vancouver with 600+ students from over 240 different universities to spend 100 days at sea visiting 10 countries. Yes, they actually got credit for this.

When she arrived in Kobe, Japan, she wrote to us about sushi and other minor trips outside the comfort zone. As the voyage progressed, however, the nature of the e-mails and phone calls changed dramatically. With visits to Vietnam, China, Malaysia, and India, she and her friends realized they were seeing the USA and their own lives from a new perspective. They would sit up late at night on the deck and talk about the gratitude they felt for the life they had.

As they continued on to Africa, Brazil, and Cuba, the nature of the conversation changed again as these young adults made some interesting observations. They noticed that everywhere they went, encountering a range of standards of living, they found smiling and happy people who cherished family and friends. This was perhaps the biggest revelation of the trip. Life may play out in a setting with or without an abundance of goods and services, but except in circumstances of true hardship, the setting in no way correlates with the quality of the human life it contains. The quality of life is a choice that can be made outside of a discussion of your 401k. A flat tire won't ruin your day if you can feel grateful, not only for the gift of transportation, but also for the gift of life.

HAPPINESS IS A SERIOUS PROBLEM

Author and LA talk-show host Dennis Prager says happiness is a serious problem. He suggests that when we rise in the morning we should notice the many blessings present each day that often go unnoticed. For example, right now your liver is very likely performing well. There is no reason you should take that for granted, but you become accustomed to a variety of important things that are really gifts. The only road to happiness is gratitude for the many blessings present in our lives. You should know that a full and happy life comes more quickly to those who find themselves swimming in a sea of gratitude. If you can create a deep sense of gratitude for the many blessings in your life you will be in the very best position to FISH!

EXERCISE

This week keep a gratitude journal, where you make daily records of the things for which you are grateful. Pay special attention to the important things you may have been taking for granted, but which could disappear in a heartbeat. Do this faithfully and by the end of the week you will be in a FISH! frame of mind. Then continue the process for the rest of your life.

In the box that follows, record some of the most interesting things you became aware of being grateful for, and share them with a friend on the weekend. By the way, don't forget to be grateful for the biggest gift of all: life itself.

> *Neat Stuff for Which I Am Grateful . . .*

Week Two: Conduct a Full FISH! Inventory and Set Some Goals

Below you will find the OfFISH!ial FISH! Scale. Look it over, and while you are doing that, think about the place where you work. Close your eyes and see the people there, watch the activity, and assess the mood on a typical day. After you have taken a good look at your workplace in your mind's eye, think about the stories in this book. Consider play at Sprint and compare your work setting to a playful, fun, light-hearted place. Think about Rochester Ford and the way they emphasize "make their day." Do the same with Missouri Baptist and ponder the way that great caregivers can learn to "be there." How does your workplace compare? Finally, revisit Tile Tech and "choose your attitude." Now complete the inventory below by circling the number that best represents how your work setting compares to the environment at the market and those described in the stories. Look at the anchor statements to guide your choices.

✗ひ
FiSH! TALES

EXERCISE: PART ONE

Play   1   2   3   4   5

1   This place is so uptight that play is a four-letter word.

5   The atmosphere here is lighthearted and playful. It brings a smile to my face just thinking about it.

Make Their Day   1   2   3   4   5

1   Customers and colleagues are treated with indifference or as an interruption.

5   Customers and colleagues are treated in a way that leaves them feeling special.

Be There   1   2   3   4   5

1   People here seem so distracted it is hard to know if they are listening.

5   You are the sole focus of attention when talking with someone here.

Choose Your Attitude   1   2   3   4   5

1   Workers demonstrate the mental maturity of a two-year-old having a bad day.

5   There is a high level of accountability, and everyone knows she or he chooses her or his attitude.

Great! Now you are ready for the hard part.

EXERCISE: PART TWO

Pick the principle whose rating you would like to improve and write a statement about it below. For example, you might write, "I chose the 2 that I gave 'Make Their Day' because I think there is a lot of room for improvement."

Now set some goals and make some commitments about what you will do this week to move that category in a positive direction. These need to be things you can do without anyone else's help. List a couple of goals to start.

Example: I will choose two coworkers and look for an opportunity to do something special for them.

Example: I will find ways to create lightheartedness in my disposition.

Now it is your turn.

1.

2.

3.

Week Three: Find Ways to Play at Work

This is an easy week. At the market they throw fish, chant, and joke with customers. At Sprint they do the Chicken Dance, take disco breaks, and celebrate each other's accomplishments. As one of the fish guys said, "There are a million ways to play. It doesn't have to be throwing a fish."

This week your job is to make a list of as many ways to play as you can think of, or until you think of 50. Remember, it is about doing things that create a lighthearted feeling at work. Observe the person who lightens the mood when they enter the room. Pretend you are an explorer in an unknown land looking for fun. Start recording your ideas and observations. I will even help you a bit.

EXERCISE:

1.   4.

2.   5.

3.   6.

7.   29. Crazy hat day

8.   30.

9.   31.

10.   32.

11.   33.

12.   34.

13.   35.

14.   36.

15.   37.

16.   38.

17.   39.

18.   40.

19.   41.

20.   42. Post family pictures in the hall.

21.   43.

22. -   44.

23.   45.

24.   46.

25.   47.

26.   48.

27.   49.

28.   50.

Week Four: Have Some Fun!

This week is dedicated to having some fun with last week's ideas. Take five of the ideas you listed last week and implement one each day this work week. If your work week is longer than five days, then "Get a life!" Just kidding. If you work Saturdays, then pick six. No big deal.

Remember that play operates in a context of "Make Their Day," "Be There," and "Choose Your Attitude." If you keep that in mind, your play will not be inappropriate. Pulling a chair out from under someone with a bad back might seem playful, but it is not likely to make that person's day.

EXERCISE

In the boxes that follow, record some of the week's highlights.

FiSH! TALES

At the end of the week, tell a colleague about your experiences.

148

Week Five: Intend to Make Someone's Day

The fish guys at the market *intend* to make someone's day every day. They have learned that when you have an intention, opportunities show up. At Tile Tech they discovered a great way to make the crew's day and have a little fun besides. Doug went out to a job site midday and surprised the crew with three motorized scooters to ride. It provided a great break in the day and a powerful message from the boss that employees are valued.

EXERCISE

Think of people in your life whose day you would like to make. List their names below, and when an idea emerges, write it down. Then, when the time is right, go for it.

FiSH! TALES

I intend to make this person's day. My idea is . . .

1. **Name:**   **Idea:**

2. **Name:**   **Idea:**

3. **Name:**   **Idea:**

4. **Name:**   **Idea:**

5. **Name:**   **Idea:**

6. **Name:**   **Idea:**

7. **Name:**   **Idea:**

Week Six: Random Acts of Kindness and Cows

After Carr Hagerman and I visited a company in Dodgeville, Wisconsin, Carr decided to rent a car (yes, his name is really Carr) and drive back to Minneapolis rather than take the plane out of Madison. When I next saw him he told me the following story.

He was on Highway 52, just outside of Rochester, Minnesota, when he saw brake lights ahead. The cause of the slowdown was soon obvious. Twelve cows were loose on the roadside and appeared ready to cross the road to enjoy the green grass in the center median. They would start across and a truck would sail by, startling them back to the side of the road, where they would build up their courage to try again.

Being a city kid, Carr saw the opportunity of a lifetime and was soon herding cows by waving his hands and yelling, "Yee-haw!" The cows moved away from the highway but remained in a dangerous spot, still blocking a sharply curving feeder road. Carr recognized the danger posed by this blind entrance and doubled his energy. Soon, all the cows were contentedly chewing their cud as they surrounded Carr on a tick-and-horsefly-infested hillside. As the cows crowded Carr, curious about his cell phone, a motorcycle piloted by a helmetless rider rocketed around the curving feeder road just a bit slower than the speed of sound, merged onto Highway 52, and disappeared into the distance.

Carr stood there—frantically scratching—thinking about the enormity of what had just happened. The young man will never know that a total stranger probably saved his life. They will never meet and exchange greetings. As the good feeling of a job well done filled his body, Carr had another thought that was a bit more humbling. "I wonder how long the list would be if it contained the names of everyone who has done something important and anonymous for me."

EXERCISE

This week is dedicated to random acts of kindness at a place they are greatly needed: at work. At the end of the week you are allowed to write down your favorite random act of kindness and tell a friend about it.

My favorite random act of kindness was . . .

Week Seven: Why Can't We Just Be Where We Are?

One of my favorite writers is a creative spirit named SARK. On my refrigerator is a colorful note card with one of her quotes. It reminds me of something so important and so easy to forget. She writes, "Why can't we just be where we are?"

The fish guys are not selling fish. They are working to improve the quality of life on the planet, one engagement at a time. And they sell a lot of fish. This is not something they could accomplish while distracted, disinterested, while talking on a cell phone or disengaged. They are present physically for their customers—and they are also present in spirit. They know how to "be where they are."

CHRISTMAS IN JULY

I once had a fascinating conversation with my friend Jerry McNellis. As a child he had polio and spent large amounts of time in Gillette Children's Hospital, in St. Paul. It was the day of the iron lung, and the Salk vaccine was just around the corner but of no help for these kids.

I didn't know Jerry when he was at Gillette, but we became friends later in life. I asked him about his time at Gillette and about the visitors who came through. During the holidays Gillette was overrun with well-intentioned people who distributed goodies and quick uncomfortable smiles as they moved through the hospital. The holidays were, for these visitors, a time to do "something" for the kids with crippling disorders. But for the kids, most of the visits were an ordeal, since they lacked one key quality: engagement. Very few of those who visited during the holidays took the time to interact with the kids. It was more like an anonymous parade with candy.

There were, however, two groups that brought the kids great joy, not just at the holidays but during the year. One was a dance troupe whose members danced with the kids. The other was a group of kids with emotional problems from St. Peter Hospital. The kids from St. Peter came in July to celebrate Christmas in July. When they visited, they played, talked, and interacted with the kids from Gillette. They were fully present. That is the power of "being there." It transforms the human dynamic.

EXERCISE

This week is dedicated to being where you are. Think of all the people with whom you interact each week at work. Consider all the work settings you visit. This activity is designed to make all of those interactions more effective, less anxious, and more pleasant.

Below are some ideas that you may either try or use to stimulate your own. After each episode, ask the person for whom you are "being there" if they would mind reflecting on the experience. This reflective feedback will help you catch any little distractions and sharpen your ability to be where you are.

"BE THERE" IDEAS:

🐟 When someone comes into your office to talk, either say, "This is not a good time," or shut down your computer monitor and un-plug or ignore your phone while conversing with the person in front of you. If you need to take a call, explain that ahead of time. Move around your desk into a good "be-there" position.

🐟 Always disclose the amount of time you have for a conversation and ask if it is enough.

🐟 When making quick exchanges in the hall, position your body so all you can see is the other person.

🐟 During conversations, clear your mind of everything but the topic at hand, then do it again and then again.

🐟 Never take a cell phone to lunch unless you are at the Motorola Technology Convention. In that case, take it but keep it off.

🐟 If you are in an open area, try not to look past the person with whom you are speaking.

🐟 Use the person's name as often as you can without getting weird.

🐟

🐟

🐟

🐟

A WEEK SEVEN BONUS: *DON'T SWEAT THE SMALL STUFF*

This week, be mindful as an aid to being there. Treat yourself by reading the delightful little book titled *Don't Sweat the Small Stuff . . . and It's All Small Stuff*, by Richard Carlson, in order to understand the power you have over distracting and negative thoughts. Thoughts can't be controlled. They will appear in your mind without warning. Your power lies not in controlling your thoughts, but in choosing not to dwell on them. You can let them go and therefore reduce the impact they have on you as you work to "be there" for another. When you apply this power you will earn an advanced degree in "be there." Take a moment to record the implications for yourself of one or two of Carlson's stories.

Week Eight: How Fascinating!
Be There Now!

For over 30 years, Tony Buzan, the creator of a system called mind mapping, has surprised and delighted audiences with two words: How fascinating! In his use of juggling as a metaphor for learning, he will drop the ball and say, "How fascinating!" His message is that dropping the ball is an important event in the learning process. Without it, learning could not occur. Rather than call it a failure or say, "Oh bleep, I dropped the bleeping ball," it is more appropriate to say, "How fascinating!", pick it up, and try again. And in learning, it is important to drop the ball well.

In a high-velocity world, "be there" is a complex skill. The distractions and pressures to take your eye off the task at hand and get pulled into the surrounding chaos are overwhelming. When it happens, you need to say, "How fascinating! I was intending to go to Charleston, West Virginia—not Charleston, South Carolina! How fascinating! I will try again."

When my first daughter, Beth, was about four years old she asked me if we could go to the park. I said sure. It was something I wanted to do, but with the heavy travel schedule I had at the time, I put it off until the next weekend. A year later I realized I had yet to take her to the park. I told this story as a part of my presentation to the American Heart Association and a week later received an e-mail from a young father of two boys. He said that for a year he had been telling his boys that he would camp out in the backyard with them. My story created an awareness in him, and he said to himself, "How fascinating! I love my boys and love doing things with them and it has been a year since we first discussed camping out in the backyard." They camped out that night.

Being there requires an awareness that penetrates the stress and chaos that is a part of our world. You will mess up, and when you do, the only reasonable thing to say is, "How fascinating!" Now try again.

EXERCISE: IN THIS MOMENT

The first assignment this week is to read this quote from Thomas Merton:

The rush and the pressure of modern life are a form, perhaps the most common form, of innate violence. To allow oneself to be carried away by a multitude of conflicting concerns, to surrender to too many demands, to commit oneself to too many projects, to want to help everyone in everything is to succumb to violence. More than that it is cooperation with violence. The frenzy of the activist neutralizes his work for peace. It destroys her inner capacity for peace. It destroys the fruitfulness of his own work

because it kills the root of inner wisdom which makes
work fruitful.

EXERCISE

Spend the rest of the week working to be one place at a time and to learn the most powerful lesson in the universe. There is little tension or anxiety in the place we call the present. And if you find yourself worrying about things in the future, say, "How fascinating!" Then take a deep breath and return to the now. And if you find yourself working on one project but thinking of another say, "How fascinating!" Then take a deep breath and choose the project that will be the sole focus of your attention. And if you find that your anxiety about everything you have to do is keeping you from going to the park with your daughter, sitting and talking to your spouse, or camping in the backyard, take a deep breath, say, "How fascinating!" and return to the now. It is a marvelous place to be. You may decide to work or you may decide to go to the park; either is just fine as long as you are wholeheartedly present. Just don't sit and be anxious. That has no value at all. How fascinating!

WEEK EIGHT BONUS: *THE POWER OF NOW*

If you find yourself wanting a little more on this important subject, let me suggest *The Power of Now*, by Eckhart Tolle. He shares such wisdom in this book that I keep it close to my desk at all times. I find that I can open it to any page and be rewarded with an insight.

Clearly, Tolle understands the damage that is caused by spending too much time in the future and the past. With great clarity he describes the peace and tranquility that can only be found when you are in the now. Open this book anywhere and enjoy. If you are like me it will stay on your desk for a long time.

EXERCISE

After you have made a few excursions into the writing of Tolle, capture some of your insights here:

Week Nine:
Do You Have a Full Deck?

I have learned a great deal from my colleague Carr Hagerman, but perhaps the most powerful lesson comes from his experience in the theatre. One day he said, "Someone who is acting is not interesting. An actor needs to *be* the person whose role he or she is playing."

I have thought a lot about this lesson from the theatre. Great actors don't "act"; they assume the emotions, feelings, and personality of the character. This to me is evidence of the power we each have to choose. Romeo and Juliet may have driven through terrible traffic and had arguments with their significant others, but you see none of that when they are onstage. We each have that capability!

In preparation for your greatest role—your own life—you might copy this idea from the theatre. Consider developing a deck of cards from which to choose your attitude. These cards would contain the name of an attitude on one side and, on the other side, words, pictures, or phrases that are helpful in producing the internal state of that attitude. In other words, "being the attitude."

If my attitude of choice is serenity, I might have a picture of my favorite listening point on Lake Superior. If patient, I can picture the quivering stillness of my dog Bo as I hold a treat in my hand. He will hold that position for hours if he needs to. If I want to create more selfless and unconditional love in my life, then a picture of Mother Teresa is perfect. If I want the attitude of wholeheartedness, then the waxing and the waning of the moon in the poem *Faith* by David Whyte will remind me that I need to have equal faith in my joys and in my grief.

EXERCISE

There are two exercises this week, and you probably have anticipated the first. Prepare the first five cards in your attitude deck. Three-by-five note cards are perfect for this task. Out of all the possible choices, pick five attitudes you would like to see more often in your life.

After you have prepared the cards, simply look at them at set intervals during the day, perhaps hourly or perhaps when the phone rings. Each time, ask yourself this question: "What attitude do I have right now—and would I be better off with one of the five in my hand?" If you don't like the one you have, choose another, but first write down the name of the one you have as best you can.

Record of Attitude Checks

The Attitude I Have: *The Attitude I Choose:*

Week Ten: It's Not about Choosing a Positive Attitude

An engineering firm in Southern California and a clothing manufacturer in the Midwest have an interesting connection. They each have produced a wall of attitude buttons from which to choose. Attached to the wall are some of the most marvelous attitudes: Peaceful, Patient, Positive, Energetic, Caring, Sensitive, Productive, and Loving. The one that is always checked out, however, is "Pissed Off."

The idea to consider this week is that it is not about choosing a *positive* attitude. It is about choosing. There will be times when the weight of life is so great that you make a less-than-spectacular choice. It is called being human. But if you can stay connected to the fact that whatever attitude you have, it is the one you are choosing right now, then the awareness itself will move you in a more satisfying direction.

Take a lesson from the Duchess and Diva of Distribution at ChartHouse. (At ChartHouse we create our own titles. It is one of the lighthearted things we do.) Wendy and Gwen manage the network of distributors for the company, a demanding task. They have a map of the world on the wall and a white board on the office door where they post their attitude each morning. I love to go by and see the daily choice. Occasionally I will see "Frustrated" or "Melancholy" written on the board, but more often it is "Confident" or "Energetic." Whatever it is, the fact that it is posted reminds the Duchess and Diva—as well as all those who walk by—that they choose their attitude. Remember, whatever your attitude at the moment, it is the one you are presently choosing.

EXERCISE

> This week's exercise is simple but powerful. Put a white board up on your office door or near your desk, and regularly post your attitude for all to see. See if your example leads others to start posting theirs below yours.

Week Eleven: Who Are You Being While You Are Doing Whatever You Are Doing? Why Not Set a World Record?

This is as good a time as any to tell you that I am a world record holder. Really! Today you might see me as bald, out of shape, 235 pounds, and in my 60s. There was a time when I was bald, out of shape, 235 pounds, and in my 50s.

In 1993, I went to Lafayette, Louisiana, to compete in the Hubba Bubba Road Race. It was the five-mile world championship for "Clydesdales." In order to qualify as a Clydesdale in the men's division, you had to weigh in excess of 200 pounds, and my 235 easily qualified me. As I lined up at the starting line I was inspired by the fact there were only five of us in my over-50 division—I could tell who the others were by the color coding on their numbers. I had already taken the measure of two competitors and felt confident they carried in excess of 250 pounds, giving them a definite disadvantage. That is, if they didn't step on my foot at the start.

The gun fired and the ground shook as the mass of meat shot from the starting line. At mile one, three of my competitors were struggling as we passed the marker in 7 minutes and 15 seconds—a blistering pace. I tucked in behind the man in fourth and dug deep into my reserves in order to hold the pace. As we approached the finish line and I prepared to go into my famous kick, my competitor stumbled over a young 300-pounder who had abruptly stopped right in the middle of the road. I raced by on his blind side and finished a full second in front of him, in a hot time of 35:40, to become world champion.

That was the last time the Hubba Bubba world championship five miler was held and so, to this day, I remain the reigning world champion. The point? If you find a small enough pond you can be a big FISH! Did you know you are not only world champion, but hold the world record for being you? And to make it even better, every time you improve on you, a new record is established. Why not shoot high?

WE ALL DO STUFF, BUT WHO ARE WE BEING WHILE WE DO STUFF?

This eleventh week is dedicated to improving the many world records you already hold. How about setting a new team-member record? Perhaps this is the week you improve your record for positive contribution to the department. This is a week to set some new world records for you.

EXERCISE

If you need a boost to get started, ask yourself, "Who would I be if I was being world-record me?" Do that for all of your major roles and keep a record of the highlights for use during your next performance review. Why not?

The Role I Am Playing . . .   *My New World Record . . .*

Week Twelve: Tag, You're It!
Light Some FISH! Fires

The first year I was a counselor at Camp Courage I was assigned to the young boys' cabin, Cabin 3. The eight- and nine-year-olds filling our cabin to the brim with energy brought with them a devastating variety of disabling conditions but a common upbeat spirit. I will never forget Beaver.

Beaver was a bucktoothed eight-year-old with muscular dystrophy. He slouched in his wheelchair because he lacked the muscle strength to sit up. On the second day of camp the ever-smiling Beaver announced he wanted to go on a hike— not on the tar paths that crisscrossed camp but through the woods. When you are a 17-year-old counselor you figure ways to do things you wouldn't consider later in life. We wrapped Beaver in beach towels to keep him safe and set off cross-country with the entire cabin in tow. Imagine a single-file line through the brush with four wheelchairs and a half dozen sets of crutches. An hour later we returned with an excited group of young boys, and Beaver could speak of nothing else. I heard that he talked about that hike all the way home at the end of camp.

The next summer I looked for Beaver's file as I prepared for the first group of campers. But Beaver had not made it through the winter. He simply grew too weak to keep going.

I think a lot about the campers who didn't come back the next summer, football teammates who didn't return from Vietnam, and other friends who have gone before me. Life is so precious, and yet we often seem as if we are passing through work on the way to another place, never really in the life we have at the moment. What a waste!

The last assignment is to live each moment fully. To live in a way that honors the preciousness of life itself. To live in a way that attracts the attention of others as they see and feel your passion for life. Perhaps your example will inspire a real conversation, and one more person will see the possibilities that follow an understanding that "life is too precious to just be passing through."

EXERCISE

Find something to wear that reminds you of your commitment to living your life fully and that causes others to comment and ask you, "What is that about?" Each time someone asks you why you are wearing an octopus on your head, or whatever, you have an opportunity to recommit to your personal vision and at the same time start a small fire in the heart and spirit of another. Over time you will find your commitment deepening.

When others ask why you are so upbeat, tell them about the choice you are making! It may help them see their own choices.

And when you are blessed with an opportunity to help

another human being to see her or his potential, take a minute to do that. It may be the most powerful legacy you leave on this earth.

It is my hope for you that you catch your limit of life— every day!

ACKNOWLEDGMENTS
AND AUTHORS' NOTE

I was considering the many and varied contributions required to produce this book when a takeoff on an old joke popped into my head.

"How many writers does it take to write a book?"

"Only one to hold the pen but it takes another twelve to move the pages."

Actually two of us held the pen on this one: Phil Strand, the "Word Wizard" at ChartHouse Learning, and me, the "Big Tuna Ph.D." Our stories came from a variety of sources. Some of the stories emerged through speaking engagements. For example, a talk at Missouri Baptist Medical Center allowed me to see all the wonderful activity firsthand and hear the story of Leo and the Conductor. Phil interviewed dozens of people at Missouri Baptist and several other organizations profiled in this book, and wrote our features. All of the stories are real, as are all of the names. We are deeply grateful to all of the daily heroes who took time to share their experiences and insights. Special thanks to Lisa Franklin, Monica Evans-Trout, Rob Gregory, and Sheila Reed for helping to arrange interviews.

Co-author John Christensen produced the documentary films we call *FISH! TALES*. These films portray real organizations using the FISH! Philosophy. All but one of the feature stories in this book was first chronicled in a documentary film. Contributing to the production of these films were Carr

Hagerman, Robb Harriss, Chris Ohlsen, Laurie McKichan, and Mark Davis.

John has organized his company, ChartHouse Learning, in a way that maximizes the opportunity to catch and record many of the stories that come to us on the phone and over the Internet. The vision of ChartHouse Learning is "Telling stories that change the world." Many of the tales can be traced back to conversations between the ChartHouse Learning staff and clients. A special thank-you goes to Cindy Amberger, Ken Chalupsky, Harry Geist, Sarah Gilmore, Gwen Heard, Wendy Koch, Jessica Kovarik, Sharon Kuubits, Anne LaDue, Rick Palmerton, Russell Peterson, Jill Schuerman, and P. J. Wester.

The ChartHouse Learning websites and FISH! Pond were developed and are maintained by our talented marketing communications team that includes Allison Donahue, Phil Hoeschen, Jackie Johnson, Patrick North, Betsy Perkins, and Mike Wilson.

The ChartHouse Learning employees who keep the place running include Robin Arndt, Kate Berning, Chuck Bragg, Loretta Engle, Pat Gurnon, Peggy Hanson, Sean Haugen, Tiew Inthirath, Kelly Julius, Kevin Mowery, Candy Sharkey, Randy Sims, Ben Tipler, and Holly Wartnick. Thanks to Kate and to Bethany Kovar for transcribing several interviews. And thanks to Mick Lunzer just for being Mick.

Co-author Harry Paul, in addition to giving his sage business advice and editing skill, went on the road this year, speaking about FISH! In between his daily workouts in the weight

ACKNOWLEDGMENTS

room, he collected stories about real people working to create a better workplace.

Others who moved the page as Phil and I held the pen include the world's best editor, Will Schwalbe (we are so lucky to work with Will), and the incredible folks at Hyperion, including Bob Miller, Ellen Archer, Michael Burkin, Jane Comins, Caroline Skinner, Jill Sansone, Corinna Harmon, Sharon Kitter, Mike Rentas, Kiera Hepford, and Mark Chait. We are especially fortunate that even though Will moved back into the executive ranks as editor-in-chief, he has continued to be a member of the FISH! team, and we continue to benefit from his wise counsel and editorial acumen. It was their fearless leader, Bob Miller, who suggested that *FISH! TALES* be the next book written.

When authors think of the perfect agent, they imagine someone like Margret McBride of the McBride Agency. We are lucky enough actually to have her as ours. Her background in publishing, her talent as a writer, and her incredible thoughtfulness have been critical to our efforts.

A final thank-you goes to three wonderful colleagues, Ray Christensen, Carr Hagerman, and Kris Brooks. Ray is the patriarch and founder of ChartHouse. He has spent a lifetime collecting the herbs and spices of great filmmaking and he passed them along to me without a second thought. When he and John invited me to join ChartHouse, they started me on the creative path that led to the writing of *FISH!* Thanks, Ray! You truly embody the meaning of curiosity, and the company you founded is a testament to that fact.

Carr has taught me to see the world through the eyes of a street performer, and the experiences that followed have been rich and rewarding, greatly contributing to this book. Kris is the last of the true believers. She has supported us with her faith, her administrative skill, and her considerable imagination.

Finally, to our families: You give us your unconditional love. What more do we need in this world?

Keep FISH!ing!
Steve Lundin
Big Tuna Ph.D.
Tahiti (kidding)
Monte Carlo (not really)
Lutsen, Minnesota, USA (you betcha)
Fall 2001

Bring the FISH! Philosophy
deeper into your organization

ChartHouse Learning has created a family of amazing resources to help you bring the many benefits of the FISH! Philosophy into your life at work. These resources include the award-winning films FISH!, FISH! STICKS, and FISH! TALES as well as books, live learning presentations and FISHin' Gear. To learn more, visit us at:

www.fishphilosophy.com

Have you been inspired by the FISH! Philosophy at work, school or home? Are you doing anything differently because of the FISH! Philosophy? If you have a story you would like to share, contact us at:

fishtales@charthouse.com

At ChartHouse Learning, our goal is to inspire people to an awareness that transforms their experience of work and life into one of deep aliveness and purpose. For more about ChartHouse learning programs, visit:

www.charthouse.com

CHARTHOUSE
LEARNING

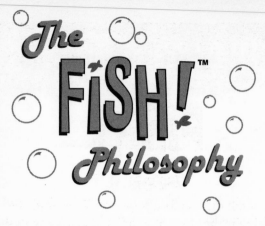

Looking for a speaker?

Are you interested in having one of the authors speak to
your organization or group about the FISH! Philosophy?
To find out about their availability, contact us at:
speakers@charthouse.com.

Want to contact the authors?

Steve Lundin:
steve@charthouse.com

John Christensen:
john@charthouse.com

Harry Paul:
harrypaul@charthouse.com

Philip Strand:
phil@charthouse.com